The Kind of Village This Is

Life in a Senior Residential Community

Donna Rankin Love

Selected passages were reprinted with permission from the following works:

Article by Art Hoppe, "Your Future Lies Ahead," originally printed in the San Francisco Chronicle.

Excerpt from *The Gift of an Ordinary Day* by Katrina Kenison, copyright © *2009, 2010*. Reprinted by permission of Grand Central., an imprint of Perseus Books, LLC, a subsidiary of Hachette Book Group, Inc.

Excerpt from Mabel Barbee Lee's *The Gardens In My Life: An Intimate Memoir*. Doubleday, 1970.

The poem "Storage" by Mary Oliver, originally printed in *Felicity: Poems*, by Mary Oliver, Penguin Books, 2015, pp. 31.

Excerpt from Anna Quindlen's *Lots of Candles, Plenty of Cake:* Random House, 2013.

Excerpt from Rachel Naomi Remen's *Kitchen Table Wisdom: Stories That Heal.* Riverhead Books, 1996.

Cover Photograph and Design by Jenny Love

To My Children

Who didn't have to struggle
to place me in a senior residence
because
I did it myself.

CONTENTS

INTRODUCTION

"GET IN THE car, Dad. We're going for a Sunday drive. You'll like it." And the desperate adult children took him to a lavish senior residence where he would receive proper, sanitary and safe, care. Ol' Dad didn't know where he was but he knew he didn't like it.

My own father, at 85, with Parkinson's Disease, frequently fell when he got up in the night and Mother couldn't lift him and didn't want to constantly call their neighbors for help, so she took him to a care center. He was strapped into bed so he couldn't get up until morning by which time he had soaked the bed. When Mother came to visit him, he was standing at the reception desk trying to check out of "the worst hotel I've ever stayed in." Mother took his arm, "Come on, Pop, we'll figure out something." She arranged for round-the-clock care until he died two and a half years later.

I was determined to avoid such sad experiences and researched senior residences in the San Francisco and Monterey Bay areas. As I toured one place with a marketing specialist, I checked the faucets for stains and leaks. I ran my hands over the finish on the front doors, squinted through windows to check "clean and sparkly." Were the blinds in good repair? Any water stains near the drain pipes under the sink? Cracks in the sidewalks? Uneven walking surfaces? Any signs of delayed maintenance? I sniffed to see if I liked the food fragrances. How well were the gardens maintained?

When possible, I slept overnight in a guest room and had a meal with residents. Did I want to be neighbors with these people?

Now that I have lived in a senior community for several years, I know I made a good decision to move before I needed help. I manage fine. I like living with elders who rarely complain of the betrayal of their bodies, and when they do, they add a splash of humor. I appreciate living more quietly, in a small space in which I feel I'm playing house.

I have adjusted to being a home-renter after 65 years of home ownership. I traded the sense of individuality that ownership gives for the security of community living. I chose to live in Santa Rosa because I found a senior community I liked. It could have been a different community in a different town. The process and experiences would be similar.

About seven months after I had moved, I wondered if others, faced with similar decisions, might benefit from my experiences. Some of you are responsible for your parents. Baby Boomers are dependent on Medicare now and will soon be faced with deciding where to spend their final years. I began to write blogs. At first, I wrote each week, then, after six months, I found once a month better.

Granddaughter Jenny Love offered to create a book of the blogs. Without Jenny, this collection that I hope will help others make the right move, would never have found completion.

Life expectancy in the United States in 1950 was 68 years; in 2017 it was almost 79 years. There are more and more of us. Elder Care is a burgeoning industry. We need to be informed and outspoken about senior services if we will be well attended.

We have a lot to learn.

These are my thoughts. I think, therefore I blog.

Donna Rankin Love
2019

The Kind of
Village This Is

1
LET'S GO

THIS PAST YEAR, 2014, has been a year of transition. Let's talk about transition.

Great transitions in my life include first day of first grade, first love, first marriage, first child...and second...and third...and finally, the fourth. Then came first divorce, first graduate degree, first post-motherhood career. Add wrinkles, first grey hair, sons' weddings, and grandchildren.

In 2013, when I was 86, I thought about moving to a senior community. I wanted to move while the moving was good, not wait until someone put me into one. I didn't want to be warehoused in an old-folks home. I wanted to join a community, to live with a sense of community. A huge transitional move from the little yellow cottage on the northern cliffs above Monterey Bay, from owning a home to renting.

These thoughts started when a friend and I visited her friend in a senior center in Santa Rosa. As Diane and I walked along the pathway to her friend's apartment, my heart leaped up and I told myself, "Pay attention." I looked about at the trees, gardens, rose bushes, low one-story clusters of apartments with little patios and bright flowerbeds. I liked the rural feel of the place. A small-town girl going home.

Next, another friend and I visited several senior residences along the Central Coast of California. Some had white table linens in the formal dining room; one served us champagne, good cheeses, and grapes; some had a lovely swimming pool; some followed up with reminders and invitations. None pulled at my heart.

So I asked the marketing director of the community I liked if I could come visit and stay overnight. That was a good idea as it gave me time to walk about and ask questions of residents. One evening I had dinner in the dining room with five resident women. I noticed one had a short wine glass. I asked her if that insulating sleeve on her glass was to keep her wine cold.

"No," she smiled, "it's to keep the glass from sliding off my walker."

I liked her inventiveness. I talked with the women and found they all were cheerful, positive, accepting, and hospitable.

In January of 2014, I sent my application and entry fee and was told that I would be notified when a unit became available, maybe in six or so months.

Surprise! In February I received a note that #16 was available and was asked when I would move. I emailed back that I was in Mexico until the end of March so it'd be at least the end of April.

And then my heart started acting up. It raced, skipped beats, beat in 3/4 time rather than in 4/4 time. I had scans and tests and was put on a beta blocker. I rested more, didn't climb so many hills, moved the computer down stairs to the main level, and drank lots of water.

Miracles began to happen. At lunch one day, I complained to a friend that I needed lots of boxes and boxes were expensive. She said, "My friend Mary just moved here from Phoenix and has a carport full of boxes she doesn't want."

"Quick," I said. "Eat up. Let's go over to Mary's."

We loaded up my car, went back for another load, and I remembered that my son Sam was coming by the next day. Sam had a truck. When he arrived, he asked, "Is there anything I can help you do?" I said, "Get in the truck. I've found a treasure load of boxes."

A new era had arrived.

2
A BOY AND A TRUCK

WHEN I WAS about twelve, impressionable, and religious, I heard the phrase "outward and visible sign of an inward and spiritual grace." I remembered that phrase last spring as son Sam and his wife Sandra stacked the collected empty boxes into the off-site storage unit in Capitola. Boxes that would contain my stuff for the move to a senior residence in Santa Rosa. My treasures, whether functional, decorative, or purely sentimental, were reminders, outward and visible signs, of friendships, loves, and experiences important to me.

During the next few weeks, I packed. Family and friends came and packed. I sorted my possessions. One stack: take. Second stack: hmmm. maybe. Third stack was out the door and onto the curb where a FREE sign dangled from the picket fence. The curb stuff disappeared by sundown day after day. People called to me through the open front door, "Do you have a bike?" and "What about a waffle iron?"

I gave the hmmm, maybe things to those who came by to help. "Help yourself." They were happy. I was happy.

Son Matt called, "Do you need any help?" As a boy in grade school, Matt, now 60, loved to pack the car the day before I drove the boys each summer from the San Francisco Peninsula to Oregon to visit relatives. Now I asked him if he'd be responsible for hiring a moving van. He would. He came over, walked through the house, measuring with his eyes. He called Penske and reserved a truck. On Saturday, April 26, 2014, he, with coffee in hand, arrived at 8:30, and drove himself and me over to the truck rental place. By the time we returned to the house, four members of our family and two strong college boys were carrying furniture and box after box out to the front yard. Matt surveyed and said, "First these and then these and then those." The truck filled up. Matt pulled down the rear door with a solid thud, climbed in, waved, and drove off toward Santa Rosa.

A boy and his truck.

Meanwhile, son John looked around and exclaimed, "I want a truck, too!" He phoned U-Haul and called out, "Come on, Mom." Daughters-in-law Joan and Holly, comfortably seated in two upholstered living room chairs in the front yard sunshine, said, "We'll get pizza while you get the truck."

John and the college boys loaded the second truck, John climbed in, lay his pizza on the seat, and drove north. Joan, Holly, granddaughter Jamie, and I thanked the strong young helpers and said goodbye to the house. Jamie had spent her 18 Christmas holidays in that beach house. Our families had celebrated dozens of events there.

After a group hug, we piled into our three cars. A parade of Love Family Women headed toward the horizon.

Are these outward and visible signs of inward grace? I think so. Surrounded by the grace of caring family and friends, a few tears, some pizza crumbs, and laughter, I moved, probably for the last time, to the senior living community in Santa Rosa, an hour north of San Francisco.

3
I LIVE IN A RABBIT HUTCH

IN APRIL OF 2014, I drove north to the senior community I'd chosen in Santa Rosa and asked myself again, "What are you doing?" and "Why this? Why now?" I thought of the houses I'd lived in during my 86 years. The first farm my father had bought was complete with one horse, one cow, one goat, a flock of dumb sheep, red chickens, black and white cats, a swarm of bees, and our dog, Bootsie. We lived there only the summer after I'd finished the eighth grade, and I think it was then that I fell in love with life in the country.

I grew up and married and as the years rolled by, the houses became larger until my husband, our four sons, and I moved into a home spacious enough for all of us and our varied interests. As the boys, one after the other, were going away to universities, their father left too, and the houses became smaller again until I lived about 18 years in a 1,100 square foot beach cottage in Capitola on Monterey Bay.

That house receded in the rear-view mirror as I headed for a 540-square-foot rabbit hutch in a senior living center. Tell me again, why was I doing this?

I knew why. I wanted to move of my own volition, not wait until I'd need to be stashed, out of the way, by my families. Difficult for them; probably painful for me. This way, I would be able to enjoy life in a community.

I tried to anticipate what it would feel like to live among old people and recalled my mother's experience when she was in her early nineties. After my father had died, Mother lived alone in their house, managing helpers, which included a gardener she fought with just once too often. She put the house on the market and moved into a retirement home. After a couple of years, she called a real estate agent and said she wanted to move out and would buy her own house in a safe community that provided managed gardeners. We asked her why she hadn't liked the retirement home. "Oh, it's full of old people. Can't even play bridge. The fourth keeps dying."

A few years later, when she was 98, she fell and cracked her pelvis. She was taken to a rehab center. Six weeks passed and she healed. She announced that she would like to stay where she was. She liked the help, the large airy room, and the bed was comfortable. We, her grey-haired children, stood around the foot of her bed and reminded her, "Mother, this is not a residence. It is a rehab center. Have you noticed people come in, get well, and leave? We'll think of something else."

She waggled her arthritic forefinger at us and commanded, "Call the manager." We did, he came, and she told him her preference. "Well, Mrs. Rankin," he answered, "that will cost you some money." She was not to be deterred. For two years she lived in her bed enjoying her windowsill lined with plants and wall-sized bulletin board of family pictures and greeting cards.

Now, today, after six months, I know what it's like to live among old people. If anyone wants to see the future, live among old people. I see women no longer able to stand up straight as they push their walkers. I watch Marie, 92, learning to drive her new red electric wheelchair as she narrowly misses running into a wall furnace. I hear Ann's cane clicking along the sidewalk as she comes to share her New York Times with me. Kaaren explains that she knows she has asked this question before, but "it's the Alzheimers," she shrugs. Rosemary, who used to body surf in Hawaii, says, "I'm disintegrating a little each day." I notice that in spite of our individual disintegration, we devote virtually no time to complaining about it. I see an acceptance and good humor as well as a hand extended to someone a little unsteady. I see residents involved in peace and justice issues. They write letters to their representatives, stand on a street corner with Women in Black, bake scones for a fundraiser.

I see Leslee, her hair carrot-colored, smiling brightly when I walk into Assisted Living for another of her bridge lessons. Leslee likes bridge and since she found no one with whom to play, she teaches bridge lessons on Wednesdays. She is 99. Mother would have liked Leslee.

We have fruit trees and rose bushes as well as small garden plots on these seven acres. Since I moved, I have grown tomatoes, sunflowers, peas, lavender, mint, and basil. Not quite a farm, not a real rabbit hutch, but close enough.

4
GENTLY GO THE DAYS

ABOUT 80 OF us live in this senior residence. I, at 87, am a bit older than some, our ages ranging from mid-sixties to ninety-nine. Most are women, with several couples living here as well as a few single men. I look to see what we have in common, why this particular group shares this address. If a guest wanders along the path and stops to ask if I know her friend, she might say, "Her name is Mary and she has short grey hair." As I write this, I can think of three Marys and they all have short grey hair. Actually, Mary or not, most of us have short grey hair. Surely there is something more we have in common.

Joanie is a peppy little lady of almost 89 who has lived here for over three years. Last week, her visiting daughter asked me if I like living here and I told her, "Yes, and even though I miss my friends in Santa Cruz County, I enjoy new friendships here. I'm still trying to figure out what makes this group unique."

She had an immediate answer. "During my adult life, I have lived in a small town and have participated in civic groups, charity groups, PTAs, and church groups. I have noticed that when volunteers are needed, the same three people raise their hands. I think people who raise their hands move here. No wonder you all get so much done!"

She may be right. Unlike other residences for the elderly, our management does not organize the musicians, speakers, and events. We residents do. One

Sunday afternoon a month, bright-eyed Betsy introduces a concert in the library. On most Tuesday and Thursday evenings, speakers entertain and inform us. Mostly the speakers are from "outside," but occasionally one of us speaks. We tell of our lives. I have told of walking across the United States in 1986 and of publishing Walking for Our Lives about the Great Peace March for Global Nuclear Disarmament.

Harriet and her library committee manage the books that are contributed. Phyllis, who moved in last spring, donated 27 boxes of books. Some were added to the library, some contributed to Friends of the (downtown) Library, and some sold on Amazon. Two years ago, the funds from Amazon sales purchased a 12-passenger bus for residents.

Nancy, an artist, moved in about the same time as Joanie. Nancy is responsible for the art exhibits along the one long hallway. She and I go to visit local artists and ask if they would hang about 20 of their pieces for two months. We explain that their work probably will not sell because we residents have very limited wall-space in our units, but their paintings will be much admired and appreciated. Every artist we have asked has said yes.

These activities require many meetings and I generally avoid meetings. If I miss something important, someone will tell me, or I can read the minutes posted in the library. Lately I've attended meetings to learn how and what people here think.

One of my favorite committees, the ripe-fruit-picking committee, doesn't have any meetings. I was asked to join because I am tall and can reach up without falling over. As the fruit ripens on our 100 trees, Ruth comes by with a couple of buckets and some clippers. "Want to pick fruit with me?" I most often do. Plums, peaches, pears, apples, pomegranates, persimmons, guavas and more are arranged on outdoor tables scattered about the property and anyone who wishes may take what they need. Joanie has baked apple cake from our apples and offered it to residents at breakfast.

Joanie's daughter is right, we raise our hands when asked. We are busy. Busy, but not harried. We have time to attend exercise and Chi Gong and Memory Enhancement. We take naps and sit on benches in the sunshine. We have time to care about each other. Our days are gentle and sweet.

5
THANKSGIVING BREAK

REMEMBER WHEN YOU left for college? All that excitement, the new clothes, the apprehension? Aaaah, away from home! Freedom! Will they like me? Will I fit in? Maybe instead, you got a job. Same feelings. Aaaah, out on my own! Freedom! Will they like me? Will I fit in?

And most likely you did just fine. You enrolled in classes you liked or you got a potted plant for your desk. After a few weeks, you wandered about a little lost. Perhaps you cried more easily in movies or when someone didn't say Good Morning. You missed your old room. You even missed your parents! You were homesick. I remember feeling a little bit homesick, but talked myself out of it. Stayed busy with classes that were lots more work than in high school.

Then Thanksgiving Break! Home again, back in my old bedroom, back at my forever place, to our father's right, at the dining table. I talked about an essay I'd written...and received an A. I played Monopoly with my brothers, helped with the dishes, wandered downtown searching for friends. The town looked smaller than I'd remembered, same cracks in the sidewalks, though. Four days later, I returned to campus and felt relieved to be back.

Last week I drove south from Santa Rosa to Los Altos and en route stopped at the Daly City BART station to pick up granddaughter Jamie, who is a freshman at St Mary's in Moraga. Like two girls heading home for the weekend, we chattered about our new experiences. I am 87, Jamie is 19 and that day we were peers. For both of us, this was the first Thanksgiving since we'd moved to our respective campuses.

I haven't asked Jamie how she feels back at school after Thanksgiving, but for me, it's a new level of comfort. Before I turned into our driveway, I saw Ann walking her dog and she waved and called out a greeting. Once parked, I walked toward my Rabbit Hutch, stopping along the way as friends welcomed me "back home."

This evening, friend Karen and I stood outside to admire the moon in skies bright after today's cleansing rain. She told me about her father who took her and her brothers outside to admire the moon. As a teenager, I hung out an upstairs window to watch the moon rise. No matter where we live, how far away we are from where we started, we have the moon. The same one. In times of transition, the moon helps.

6
MEASURE AND MOVE

BY APRIL OF 2014, I had moved from my cute little cottage in Capitola to a retirement community in Santa Rosa…into less than half the space, from 1100 square feet to 540. I would have to be very selective about what possessions I'd bring along. My first step was to measure the furniture I wanted to keep. Then I drove up to Santa Rosa, met son Sam, and we began measuring Unit 16. Sam was in the living room with his paper, pencil, and tape. I was in the bedroom with my tape stretched along the wall between two doors.

"Ratz! Two inches too narrow," I muttered. "Now what'll I do? I was counting on placing that tall chest of drawers here."

From the other room, Sam said calmly, "You could buy something."

What an great idea! I had been thinking of the furniture I had as pieces of a jigsaw puzzle that had to fit into #16. I was stunned by Sam's suggestion, stepped back and absorbed the wonderment that I could *buy* a piece of storage furniture for tee shirts and sweaters, socks and underwear.

When I returned to Capitola, I drove to Crawford's Antique Furniture Warehouse. They buy wooden country pieces from Pennsylvania, repair them, leave the old color and dings alone. I already had an orange cabinet for the TV and two chimney cupboards. When I arrived, John Crawford offered his help. I told him, "I need something with shelves behind a door and a couple of drawers." I told him the size. He walked me over to a charming old yellowish piece; two drawers above a wide, single door hiding four shelves. "Probably early 19th century," he said and measured it. "Perfect," I said. "Could you bring it over to the house in a couple of weeks?"

John pocketed his tape. "Fastest sale I've ever made. See you in two weeks."

The tall stack of drawers is saved in a commercial storage unit on Santa Rosa Avenue, full of things I might need someday. In my bedroom on top of the sort-of-yellow cupboard, I have arranged three old yellow ware mixing bowls left from the substantial collection I used to have. I lie in bed and admire the combination. Who ever heard of mixing bowls in the bedroom? Well, now we have.

7
CHOOSING CHEERY

LAST THURSDAY, SANTA Rosa had 4 inches of rain in 24 hours. Very wet, but not as destructive a storm as anticipated. Prior to heavy rain, schools and some roads were closed. Warnings interrupted Christmas music on the radio. A friend and I canceled a Great Peace March presentation in Mendocino because we heard of possible power outages. Seems everyone was worried. I wondered if I should keep or cancel a dental appointment and then suddenly remembered: I grew up in Oregon. I know how to drive in the rain, even after 60+ years as a Californian. I went. There was little traffic, no outages. Life went on. A choice. Stay or go. Live life or stay under cover.

In the evening, before going to bed, I stepped out my door to watch the rain splattering on the walks between our buildings. The air was warm, there was no wind. I thought everyone else was fast asleep. As I watched, I noticed Jay, in her raincoat and hat, standing out in the rain, looking all around. I got an umbrella and walked to her. "What are you doing up so late?" I asked.

She grinned and lifted her arms. I thought of Gene Kelly in Singing in the Rain. "How could I close my eyes when all this is going on!" We stood in the glittering rain and chatted until she said, "You haven't seen my apartment. Come on in and I'll show you." It's fun to see the various ways we treat our similar spaces. Jay's is full of books, some art, an antique dining/work table, a dresser displaying a Chinese urn. In the bathroom we stood before a cork board and she pointed out pictures of friends and spoke of those who have died.

She also told me that she's lived here for sixteen years. When she entered, the fee was $400 a month; now it is $2,200. She used to worry about the increased rent. Now Jay shrugs and says, "Well, so I'm spending my savings. What am I saving it for now?"

We can be frightened by the thought of a possible storm or we can choose to be singing in the rain late at night.

Guess what I choose. What about you? Cheery?

8
THE VOID

WHAT DO YOU prescribe for loneliness? How do you get over it? After more than a week with friends and family in their various San Francisco Bay Area homes, I returned to my community in Santa Rosa. I have plodded through the days, eating too much chocolate, gazing at the new photos on the fridge, yearning for more of the warmth and affection shared with people I've known a long time.

I miss the convenience and comfort of knowing where to find New Leaf Market on 41st Ave in Capitola, and once inside, knowing where to find the cinnamon. I like to know where to find parking when I meet friends for lunch. I miss Sue, Mary Pat and Jan, Connie, Cathy and Barbara and Marsha and Suzanne. Some of us are left-overs from a writing workshop we took together more than 15 years ago. When that series ended, we formed a book club to read with a writer's POV. We are now more than a book club; we are durable friends.

Here, I have new acquaintances. Residents are friendly, supportive, and kind.

I miss the hugs and hand-holds, pats and understanding glances of my families. Five grandchildren are in their 20s, one is 19, two in their 30s. Granddaughter Jenny snuggles up to swing hands with me, her sister Sarah leans her shoulder into mine and announces, "I've been accepted at NYU!" Son John holds a door open for me and smiles when I meet his gaze. Jamie opens her arms and sprints toward me, "Gran! I'm glad to see you!" On and on. I miss the easy laughter, the give-and-take. I want more!

I am fortunate to have son Sam and his wife Sandra, and Sandra's mother Betty nearby. We see each other frequently and will watch the Rose Bowl Game together. Sam and I will root for our alma mater, University of Oregon, as we sit shoulder-to-shoulder, family-style.

I do have confidence that there is Life after Christmas. The void will fill and I'll pass by the photos on the fridge with a smile of appreciation for my good fortune. But, first, I'll just have this last bit of chocolate-peppermint candy that Katie gave me on Christmas morning.

9
PICK YOUR PEOPLE

"SO, DONNA," FRIENDS asked last month when I visited in Santa Cruz, "what have you learned since April when you moved? How do you like living in a community?"

"First, I've learned I enjoy living in a play house, in a rabbit hutch." No matter where I stand, if I need the screw driver or hammer or anything else in the utility closet, it is no more than 10 steps away. I have learned I don't shop and accumulate as I have in the past. I'm not the saver I used to be. Keep it simple is a good motto. The space is adequate. I've learned it's the people. The people are the most important.

The staff makes life easy. They serve optional meals in the dining room. Someone comes to clean the apartments every two weeks. Gardeners appear on Mondays. A repair man comes when I report my furnace not working on a morning when the outside thermometer says 27 degrees.

However, I believe the most important facet of living in a senior community is who already lives here. Before I moved in, I met several residents I liked. Now I realize that the residents are not just a little bit important, but profoundly important. Residents *are* the community. Choosing a community is as important as choosing a college roommate.

So when searching for your final address on this earth, check out the people who live where you are looking. Do cliques prevail? What is the discussion at dinner? What are their politics? Similar to yours? Do you hear gossip and whining or do most seem happy and kind?

Something else you might do is to look over the magazines on the coffee table in a commons room. The magazines here include *The New Yorker, the Atlantic, Harper's, Scientific American, Smithsonian, Earth Island Journal, Teaching Tolerance, The Sun, London Review of Books.* What types of people read magazines such as these?

Just as I have perused books on a new friend's shelves to learn about her interests, I looked at the collection in the community library. After I'd noted the many biographies, books on the arts, social issues and politics, some on history, and a wall of fiction, I asked, "Where are the mysteries?" The resident who volunteered in the library that day, motioned me to walk with her down the hallway to a sitting room. There, in several tall bookcases, were many mysteries. The volunteer explained, "Our librarian decided to put the mysteries here so we'd have more room for the books contributed by new residents who move in with boxes of too many books."

I mentioned to friends who don't yet live in a senior community that my intention is to not constrict my life, but to live fully, as has been my habit. Life may be grayer and quieter, but I have chosen a good place to live among residents I can love. I may be a little scared, but at the same time, I am excited about the future.

10
KIND TO THE KIDS

ON ONE OF our Saturday morning walks, friend Ruth said, "I'm being kind to my kids."

"Oh? How? What have you done?"

"I've gone to an attorney and we've created a trust. I have trustees. The assets are divided and explained. Signed and delivered." Her arms flew up in a free gesture.

"That's such a big job," I said. "I didn't realize there would be so many decisions and details to deal with, but mine's done, too. All in place. What a relief!"

We stopped to watch some ducks, three pairs, paddling along Santa Rosa Creek.

She asked, "How are you dividing your possessions?" and I told her I'd given away, and continue to give away, things I think people in my family might enjoy. "I had a few strands of pearls from my mother and wanted the granddaughters, her great-granddaughters, to have them, but there weren't enough necklaces to go around. So I took them to a bead shop and the woman there offered to make eight necklaces with pearls separated by gold chain. I drew sketches of the different arrangements, divided the pearls into little baggies and wrote the names of the granddaughters on the sketches and baggies. She made eight individual necklaces, all with my mother's pearls, and I give them to each granddaughter as she graduates from university. I still have three to go."

Ruth and I talked about putting stickers on paintings and furniture to designate the recipient. We talked about the families gathering and drawing numbers to take turns choosing. All we are trying to do is set out our cookies so the distribution will be fair. I told about a son who had asked that I make a "Wish List," to inventory everything, list it, and write the recipient's name next to each item on the list. "I tried that, but didn't get very far. My hope is that by the time my family has to share or shed the possessions, there won't be much more than my toothbrush, hairbrush, and Chapstick to discuss. I want peace in our family, but just as I told my sons when they were boys, I'll tell them in the will, 'if you're going to fight, go outside!' Usually, by the time they got outside, the steam had sort of dissipated."

We ambled along, kicking crunchy leaves and talking about the care we receive. "Our children should know that we wear alarm devices, that there is a call box on the bathroom wall with a fairly long pull cord, and that the staff in skilled nursing is on duty 24/7 so we can call them if we fall. No need to worry about us."

Ruth added, "We also could tell our kids about the *Day Signs*. They need to know that the volunteer residents check them each morning to see if they have been changed, that they show we are up and know what day it is, and that we are okay." Barbara, across the walk from me, has been checking her neighbors at nine o'clock every morning for seven years. Sometimes I forget to change my sign in the window and she rings the doorbell.

Ruth and I ended our walk with plans to walk again the next Saturday. "Let me know if you think of something else we might tell our kids…like the Do Not Resuscitate papers and all that stuff," she said.

"I'm working on that, but for now, I don't think our children are worried about us. Well, I hope they aren't."

11
GIVE YOURSELF AWAY

IN THE GROUP that meets each weekday morning at eight o'clock in Marie's apartment, we currently are reading *The Art of Happiness in a Troubled World* by His Holiness The Dalai Lama and Howard C. Cutler, MD. Have you noticed that scientific research and the new Positive Psychology movement are defining happiness and studying the means of achieving it?

For a long time – ever since I first became enthralled with Mexico in 1988 – I have noted that although Mexicans have their social problems, loneliness is not one of them. In that culture, family comes first. And many Mexicans have large families. Frequently three or four generations live in one home. By contrast, we Norte Americanos, in our separate homes, in our individual cars, valuing our independence and privacy, are so lonely we pay someone to listen to us. The Dalai Lama reports that 25% of United States population has no one to listen to them talk about something important. Many isolate themselves in front of TV. With our mobility, young families move away; grandparents move to senior centers. Our e-communication devices weaken social ties.

We yearn for the warmth of community, a sense of involvement, a spirit of cooperation. Our general malaise, our sense of vague unhappiness, leads to mild chronic depression. First, we must become aware of our feeling of alienation. Then what do we do? I say, "get involved." On the Great Peace

March in 1986, when no fewer than 400 of us walked from Los Angeles to New York to Washington, DC, I experienced a sense of involvement, of contribution, as never before. We depended upon each other, helped each other, cheered for each other as we bounced along 15 to 25 miles a day. Actually, at the time, I didn't focus on our sense of community. But later, about 25 years later, as I was writing the book, *Walking for Our Lives*, about the experiences of walking for nine months to bring down nuclear weaponry, I realized that the reason I had had such a good time, that I had felt so supremely great, was that I had been living in a tight, dedicated community. I was involved with a wide variety of people who were making a contribution to the world! That's a very good sense of well-being! Even in driving rain, leaky tents or summer weather hot enough to melt the asphalt; the discomfort, the rice and lettuce meals, the crowds, the lack of bathing facilities…none of that wiped away the deep satisfaction of actively belonging to a community. That feeling led to good humor, even silliness, generosity, flexibility, a sense of security and safety, compassion, and empathy. That sense of community was our anchor, our rootedness. The sense of community brought out the best in us. Most of us, anyway.

So, two years ago, I asked myself what do you want to do in the next epic of your life? I silently shouted, I want to live in a community!

I've found what I wanted in Santa Rosa. The residents care for each other and care for people around the world. We have a zest for life, are emotionally involved. We dare to love those who will surely die. We laugh easily. Well, most of us do. We are generous, flexible, considerate. We live at the intersection of compassion and empathy. We are happy people. Most of us. Those who are excited.

Many of you are already involved and know what I'm saying. To you who are not, I urge you to contribute to your local community, to someone who needs you. Share. Give yourself away. Be extravagant. I think your happiness quotient will rise. What would that feel like?

12
WHAT'S YOUR HURRY, HARRY?

AS I WALKED a pathway this morning, nostalgia surged within me and tears almost over-flowed. I stopped, sucked in my breath. What had caused that moment? I sniffed. Something sweet. Squinting against the bright sunlight, I followed the fragrance and there, in the shadow under the eaves of the Assisted Living building, was a Daphne bush in new bloom. I bent down closer to it and suddenly I was nine years old in our backyard on Coulter Street and taking out the garbage, my job that spring. Next to the garbage can was a luxuriant Daphne plant.

This morning, almost 80 years older, I recalled my brothers on the swings, sheets flapping on the clothesline. I felt the cool air of southwestern Oregon. I heard our mother in the kitchen whistling a little 1936 tune as she peeled potatoes for dinner. As I had then, this morning I inhaled Daphne fragrance and almost wept at the sweet purity of it.

I resumed my walk and whispered, "Thank you for that."

At a community meeting on Sunday, Clare told us that on her way she had noted something she felt is important. Clare is a poet, a thoughtful, observant woman with impaired eyesight. She said, "I was walking along quickly to get here and caught up to Meg in her wheelchair. We greeted each other and Meg said, 'You don't have to wait for me. I'm pretty slow.'"

Clare continued, "I realized that if I hurried on, I would miss the opportunity to be in the company of a lovely human being. I slowed, and thought, This must be part of our wisdom.

When we give ourselves time, we can see and appreciate what we have at that very moment."

I agree with Clare. When we walk, we have time to breathe, to smell... see...feel...to listen. On the Great Peace March across the United States in 1986, for nine months I did just that. My original idea, to tour our country from on foot, was a good one, but as we continued day after day, I evolved.

In my book, *Walking for Our Lives*, about this adventure, I recount, "I had time to pause and watch the horses. There must have been 30 of them in their pasture along the road. They got as close as they could to us, then whirled and thundered back along the fence, only to turn again, and race to catch up. They whinnied and snickered and strained against the fence. A few marchers crossed over to pet them. Then the horses turned like a flock of birds in flight to run back and forth yet again. What were they thinking? My tears welled up at their magnificence." I still wonder about those creatures on a sunny morning in Nebraska when I was taking the time to walk.

Here, where I now live, I heard resident Maryanne make a similar observation about slowing down. Only it had to do with her electric car. She said, "The car can leap from zero miles an hour to 60 miles an hour in a flash, but when the battery is low, it will go only 25 miles an hour. Slowing down expands its range."

What a lesson!

13
LIKE A BOX OF CHOCOLATES

LIKE A BOX of chocolates, each one waiting to be chosen, the sixty-or-so residents looked up expectantly when I stood at the microphone and said, "Good Evening! Welcome to our Birthday Party. This celebration is for those who had birthdays in December and January."

I was – imagine, me! – the master of ceremonies. There's always a first time, and this was certainly the first time in my 87-year long life that I'd agreed to be the MC. Joanie of the birthday party committee had said, "You can do it. I'll give you a script and you just follow it." Fortunately, I wasn't required to wear the colored paper hat shaped like a multi-layered birthday cake adorned with paper candles. I had balked at that. "Oh, no," I'd said. "I'd feel like a clown and I'm not good at that. Not the hat!"

On Wednesday, the day before the party, I had spied resident Michael working a jigsaw puzzle. I stopped to ask him, "Are you ready to lead a few songs tomorrow evening? Did someone give you the song sheets?"

Michael thought a minute. "You know," he said, "my memory is not so reliable any more. I'm sure someone did, but I don't need the song sheet. I have songs written in a small book. I'll use that."

I explained that it'd be good to use the song sheet as that is what the audience would have. "When you find it, choose about three songs, and we'll all sing together."

"All right," he patted my arm, "I'll do that," and he returned to the array of puzzle pieces.

Thursday evening, I followed the script and introduced the 13 honorees. Michael led us in singing Happy Birthday. With the song sheet in hand he burst into Drink to Me Only With Thine Eyes on page one. When the song ended, someone called out, "Let's sing Yankee Doodle on page five." Michael, flustered by the new idea, flipped pages. From the back row, an enthusiastic male voice started and others followed while Michael, looking determined, sang along. As soon as he could, he suggested Auld Lang Syne. Then, awash in his success, he began, "You Are My Sunshine." When it ended, he looked to me for approval.

I nodded affirmation to him, applauded, stood up, and thanked him. He grinned and said, "Is that all? I have more."

"Good, Michael. You were great. Another time. Thank you." And everyone clapped and called out thank you to him. "Yea, Michael!"

I looked at the sweet, happy, timeworn faces. Everyone was having a good time. Chocolates nestled in a candy box.

In her earlier life, Bev was a public school teacher and a professional clown. She still tap dances. She came to the microphone to explain the game of Clues. "Someone will read three clues about a birthday person. The first clue won't be much help, but if you think you know who the birthday person is, raise your hand. Don't tell us! Then we'll hear a second clue, one that may be familiar to some. Don't tell us! Just raise your hand. Then, the third clue will make the mystery person obvious. When we've guessed who it is, I'll ask for more details about one of the clues and we'll find out more about that person's life. Got it? Here we go. Kaaren, are you ready? What's the first clue?" For over half an hour we played the Clues game. Chocolates chosen, one after the other. Lots of cross-talk, much laughter.

Several wished to speak at Open Mic, and one-by-one I called on them to come up to read a poem, tell a story, relate an experience. Steve shared Some Great Truths that Adults Have Learned: Raising teenagers is like nailing jelly to a tree. Wrinkles don't hurt. Families are like fudge…mostly sweet, with a few nuts. Laughing is good exercise…it's like jogging on the inside.

Still laughing, I announced, "We have concluded this portion of our party, but we're not through yet. Ice cream and cake are waiting for us in Commons B. Happy Birthday, Everybody!"

Volunteer residents had set the tables with pastel colored cloths and centerpieces of flowers. We had ice cream, cake, coffee, tea, and apple juice and just as we did at parties 70 or 80 or even 90 years ago, we babbled excitedly.

I'm always surprised that we who see each other almost every day have so much to talk about. But on the other hand, we have celebrated many years. We have not spent our lives lined up like chocolates in a pretty box.

14

GETTING THERE

AN OUTING. A field trip. Experiential learning. A Day Trip. On ferries, light rail, BART, a bus, ACE, the Metro, Amtrak, Caltrains.

If I weren't living in this community in Santa Rosa, I might never have heard about this excursion, but Steve lives here, too, and for 12 years has been actively promoting, lobbying for, and campaigning for the building of SMART train to run initially from Santa Rosa to San Rafael. Part of that promotion is to familiarize Bay Area residents with public transportation. "It's fun," he says. So Steve led four of us on a fam (familiarization) trip. We drove to Larkspur Landing where we boarded a ferry and arrived about eleven o'clock at the Ferry Building in San Francisco.

Thinking ahead to the lunch crowd, we ordered box lunches at Delica, a sort of Asian Fusion restaurant, and told them we'd be back. A nice walk a few blocks up Market Street and we hopped on SF Municipal Transit system's light rail N Judah car to the Caltrain Depot at 4th and King Streets. And back again. At Delica, we picked up our Asian lunches, sat at a community table, and I giggled that an Asian man next to us was enjoying an old fashioned hot dog. San Francisco at its best; a melding of cultures.

We took the ferry across the Bay beyond the spans of the Bay Bridge to Jack London Square in Oakland. A broad sidewalk passed the fragrant Miette Patisserie where Teri and I wordlessly veered in perfect unison through the door to buy treats. Then onto an Amtrak Capitol Corridor train south as far as Santa Clara and the Levi's stadium where the San Francisco 49ers play. While we waited for a north-bound double-decker train to take us to Pleasanton, I walked over to the stadium just because it was there and thought how well balanced this outing was: some riding and then some walking and then some riding again.

Back on Amtrak, we passed the Morton Salt Flats northeast of Santa Clara on Leslie Avenue and wondered why one salt company was on an avenue named for another salt company. Up through the soft green hills of Niles Canyon; a pair of tunnels, one 2000 feet long, opening to far views. A short bus ride and then BART under the bay to Embarcadero Station. Teri said, "If we hurry, we can make the 6:30 ferry back to Larkspur Landing." Steve held his hand aloft, "Use your ticket here to get out through these gates." I fumbled in my pocket for my ticket. I showed Chip the tickets I found. "Nope. Wrong ones." He offered his hands to hold everything I took out of my purse. A woman's nightmare.

Steve motioned me to follow him, he on the outside, I stranded inside, the others in limbo. At a booth, Steve talked, motioned, and pointed toward me. The agent, bless him, signaled me through an emergency exit. We scurried down Market Street. Chip pushed Chris in his wheelchair. I hoped my 87-year-old lungs would not burst and remembered an African proverb: When you pray, move your feet. We crossed the traffic lanes, and into the Ferry Building. Out the other side, down the ramp, to the gates. I clutched my ticket, slid it across the sensor at the gate. It set off harsh buzzers. A nearby agent shook his head, "This is only a one-way ticket. You go over there to get a new one." Steve dashed to the ticket dispenser, Teri pushed through the gate and ran up the ramp to ask some official to please hold the ferry for us. I stood stunned, harried commuters surging around me. All day long we had made all the connections, had enjoyed a smooth tour. Now this. The agent saw that Steve was having trouble with the ticket dispenser so waved me through. Then it was Chris's turn. His ticket set off the buzzer again. And so did Chip's. By then Steve had tickets for them and we hustled up the ramp and onto the ferry. We were the last passengers to board! Whew!

Forty minutes later, as we drove north from Larkspur Landing, Chris, recently retired and looking forward to new adventures, said, "I've been wanting to use public transportation, but didn't have a clue about how to do it. Now I know. How often do you have these trips, Steve?"

"Oh, about three times a year. People from all over join us. Those from the Peninsula often meet us at 4th and King Street or at the Ferry Building.

You can email Friends of SMART: friendsofsmart@sbcglobal.net to find out more."

I offered, "I think you could charge more. All those fares and lunch and your taking care of everything for $70? It's a bargain. And you're right. Public transportation is exciting. Sometimes stressful, but fun."

15
MAKE THE HOUSE COMPLETE,
ONE MORE TIME

THIS TIME IT'S all for me. Just me. Living in 560 square feet doesn't provide much space for others. Oh, I keep beer in the fridge in case son Sam comes by. I still buy a chunk of white cheddar because son Matt has always gone for the cheese and crackers. But if I want to arrange an assortment of 12 small paintings and a green leaf wreath on the same wall as the thermostat, I can. I did. I don't need anyone else's approval.

Well, it is a rental, so I'm restricted in a few ways, but not unreasonably so. The management says I can make any changes as long as I agree to pay to put it back the way it was when I moved in. I agreed and Sam took the door off the pantry closet. He grunted and said, "Call the front office, Mom, and tell them there's an interior door leaning against the swamp pump in your back area. It's gonna rain. They should come get it."

If I'm addicted to anything, it's shelves. I like the accessibility to the shelves in the open pantry, now painted an acid green and the door frame a dark barn red. I like the 1 x 12 shelf that spans the space above two doors in the bedroom and another above the large window in the living room. I can see treasures that I seldom use, sacred relics of travels and gifts from people I love...or have loved.

"To make the house complete." A family phrase. As children, my brother John and I made little forts and tiny shacks in a grove of trees near our growing-up home. We foraged for pieces of plywood, a scrap of carpeting, a refrigerator box, and created our shelter. Then we'd hunker down inside, look around, and grin. Eighty years later I have that same pleasure as I look around this tiny space where I live.

I live with my favorite possessions. One day about 50 years ago, as I was driving the young sons back home from a visit in Oregon, we stopped at a gas station near Redding. I spied a table lying out in the weeds of an empty lot. No top, but the frame, legs, and a drawer were intact. Matt helped me tie it onto the car. I hired someone to make a top for it and it's been a project table, a dinner table, a side table, and now it's my writing table.

Nearby hangs a small splint basket that holds keys and my sunglasses. I remember buying it in Kentucky in 1986 when tent-mate Shelah and I were wending our way back to the West Coast after walking nine months to Washington DC with the Great Peace March for Global Nuclear Disarmament. We had her car, which had been used on The March for errands, and Shelah had said, "Whatever you buy must be small or you'll have to ship it home." I had admired her forthrightness and had bought small.

In his highly recommended book, *Being Mortal*, Atul Gawande, surgeon at Brigham and Women's Hospital in Boston, professor at Harvard Medical School, discusses the challenges of elder-care. Medically, the goal is to efficiently keep us safe.

Even more important, he feels, is to replace the sterility of institutions with the serenity of a home atmosphere. When my mother elected to live out her remaining months (as it turned out, about 27 months) in a rehab center, she had a table moved from her home into her room. She insisted on another table, child size, and two small chairs, as well as a box of toys. A six-year-old wrote, "Great Grandmother Rankin is a very old lady. She lives in her bed. She has lots of toys."

The marketing person phones to ask if she may show my Rabbit Hutch to a prospective resident, I say "yes." When they arrive, I listen to her explain that we who live here are encouraged to create our own home. Dr. Gawande should come see.

16
LET'S TRY THIS!

ON WEDNESDAY MORNINGS, a bright-eyed young woman, Ginger, arrives to lead us in a class of Memory Enhancement. This week Ginger gave the six of us a list of 120 physical sensations. She asked us to circle words that described how we were feeling. I circled five: cool, firm, solid, thick, strong. What am I, a tree stump? Some circled a dozen sensations.

Ginger then asked us to list ten things for which we are grateful. Some of us could think of three or four; I thought of 21 and only stopped because the time was up. Did I have many because at the end of each day I habitually list my gratitudes? That's what my friend Diane used to call them, her gratitudes. Each evening she made notes on a calendar reserved for that purpose. I don't use a calendar, but I do say thanks for the gifts of the day.

I am grateful for good health, for my family, for enough, mild weather, full moons, the ring-walk around our buildings. I'm excited about the daffodils that will bloom next week to announce early Spring. I'm thankful for the kindnesses and generosities of others, for their sense of humor. I love colors and friends and music and salted almonds and long memories, a sense of safety. I'm glad I can smell paperwhites and taste Roquefort cheese, am able to see and to hear. And have a massage every two weeks.

When I told friend Betty about the list, she said she is grateful she can brush her teeth without having to take them out.

The second part of our Memory Enhancement exercise was a Walking Meditation. We walked slowly, heel-toe, mindful of our feet on the floor, aware of our breath. One step on the in-breath, one step on the out-breath. Alert to how our bodies felt. After 18 steps, we were to stop and think of something for which we were grateful. Then start the walk again. We were to focus. Ginger said, "If you focus, pay attention, you'll be able to remember better."

Sure enough, after the Walking Meditation, I could underline 17 physical sensations: alert, depth, dizzy, energized, expanding, heavy, intense, moving, quivery, sense of substance, shaky, slow, taut, trembly, vivid, wobbly, whole. I noticed that it's more difficult to balance while walking slowly. I added to the gratitudes that I'm grateful for a secure upbringing. And two tall good-looking former husbands.

The homework assignment is to choose a mindfulness exercise. We may choose making tea, tying our shoelaces, washing our hands, brushing our hair, taking a walk, or folding laundry. Yvonne and I have chosen washing our hands because it's something we do frequently. We are to perform our task mindfully, being conscious of our body and mind while remaining aware of the task.

In class next week we will describe the sensations experienced during our task. I remember how blessed I felt on the Great Peace March one morning as I stood next to our frosty tent with a very warm wet washcloth on my face. Maybe washing hands will become a sacrament.

I think the overall lesson here is that if we pay attention, really focus, are mindful, we will improve our memory. Want to try it? Can't hurt, might help. Let me know. Don't forget!

17
WHAT DO WE HAVE HERE?

WEDNESDAY EVENING I joined nine other residents at a home concert in Vera's apartment. Barbara and Vera take turns once a month hosting a musical evening. They leave a sign-up sheet in the lobby and because of space, limit the attendance to ten. Each person brings a snack: cheese and crackers, popcorn, Mrs. See's chocolate-covered raisins, salted nuts, apricot-chocolate-nut bread from Gayle's Bakery in Capitola.

Vera started the CD, turned off the lights, and we sat quietly in the dark submersed in Beethoven's "Piano Quartet, Op 16" (Emanuel Ax, piano; Isaac Stern, violin; Jaime Laredo, viola; Yo-Yo Ma, cello). After a lilting Vivaldi, we enjoyed the intermission snacks and Vera's warm apple cider. Then we settled down for Brahms' "Double Concerto" with Herbert von Karajan conducting the Berlin Philharmonic Orchestra.

I, sated with chocolate, awash in symphonic music, and surrounded by friends, sat there in the dark and thought of some of the ways in which we here care for each other.

Last week Betsy stopped by to ask if I liked parsley. She had a sprig of large flat-leaf parsley to show me. When I told her yes, she grinned and said, "I'll pot up some for you and leave it outside your front door." Next morning, there it was, with all its green vigor.

Charlotte called to me. I stopped pulling weeds and she came over, "I just want you to know I pruned your roses and left some plant food by your faucet. I'm hoping you can feed them." We'll have healthy roses this year; one is the award-winning Peace Rose.

Marion phoned, "I remembered you said your goal is to walk all the creek paths in Santa Rosa so I called the Chamber of Commerce and asked for a map. They have sent a very good one and we can mark off the areas we want to walk next." Marion, Nancy, Ruth, Elspeth, and I walk most Saturday mornings.

Ruth knocked and pushed open the door a crack. She called out a yoo-hoo, came in, and sat in the rocking chair. She waved two old-fashioned round cake pans. "I borrowed these from Joanie," she said, "And I'm going to make a birthday cake for John like his grandmother used to make. Want to come to dinner tomorrow? Do you eat shrimp? We could have scampi." You bet!

Joe is our computer tutor, a resident who is on call at all reasonable hours. Whenever I have e-trouble, I call Joe and he comes right over, fiddles around, mutters to himself, and then announces, "It's okay now." Sometimes I feel that I might be imposing and hesitate to call him, but his wife Joan says he likes helping people. "It's part of his service," she says.

I overheard Dorothy, who still drives, saying to Marie, who doesn't, "I haven't gone to the market yet today, but I will in a couple of hours so before I leave, I'll come by to get your list."

The other day Nancy said "I've renewed my driver's license, but it won't arrive for a few weeks so I can't drive. Would you take me to the dentist's office? I'll walk home afterward." Of course.

As I passed through the lobby to mail some letters, Sally called out from the wing chair where she waited for friends who were coming to lunch. When they arrived, she took a box from them, handed it to me, and asked, "Would you like to look through my father's Beatrix Potter books? Mrs.. Tiggywinkle, Peter Rabbit, Squirrel Nutkin. They're all here." Little did she know that Beatrix Potter is one of my favorite people; a writer and sheep farmer whose life inspired my dreams of becoming a combination writer-farmer. I brought her father's books back to my "Rabbit Hutch," sat in the sunshine, and read and read those treasured little stories.

However, life here is not perfect. We are bound to have disappointments and differing points of view. The rents will increase three to five percent each year, which I've learned is normal. Not as bad as the 30% increase right after I'd moved in. We residents are worried that no care is available for those with severe memory loss. Maybe that will be included in the proposed expansion plans, which are, in themselves, causing concern. I was told, "No, a nurse will not come help you if you fall down. Call 911 for the ambulance to take you to the hospital."

But multiply the random acts of kindness by 80 residents and we are mostly what I was looking for. A community.

18
JENNY'S VISIT

GRANDDAUGHTER JENNY, 23, arrived from Berkeley with a bundle of sunflowers, my favorite flower, after tulips. She had come to visit and spend an overnight. We chatted a bit and then drove the 12 miles to Sebastopol as I needed to deliver another copy of my book, *Walking for Our Lives*, to Copperfield's Bookstore for their Local Authors shelf.

As we returned to Santa Rosa, she asked if I'd seen all the Oscar contenders and I said, "Some. There's a movie theater on Summerfield." So we pulled to the curb across the street from the movies and read the marquee. Mr. Turner, I nodded. "I've been wanting to see that. It's about a 19th Century English painter. I've seen his work in the British Museum in London." Jenny checked her phone for the show times. "It starts in 20 minutes." She parked the car, took my hand, as I had taken hers so long ago, and we walked quickly, illegally, across the street.

Afterward, we shared our thoughts about the film. In the car, she asked, "Are you hungry, Gran?" and we decided to go to our favorite Thai restaurant. There, I ordered a glass of Pinot Grigio and Jenny lighted up. "That's my favorite wine. I'll join you." That's a first. I'd never seen her with wine. We clinked our glasses and agreed that, for us, William Turner was not a likable man, but he surely could paint tumultuous skies.

Back in my Rabbit Hutch, we unfolded the hide-a-bed, found the peachy-colored sheets for it, took turns in the bathroom. Jenny said, "We were gone the entire day! Good night, Gran. Sweet dreams."

We wakened at about the same time, had our favorite oatmeal breakfast, and turned on the computer. When Jenny was not much more than a toddler, before she could speak clearly, she played games on the computer, which, I think, is probably true for everyone in her generation. After she taught me some computer tricks, it was time for her to leave.

We walked out to her car in Visitor Parking, and she was seated behind the wheel as we said our final goodbyes. I glanced up at the hills to the east of Santa Rosa and for a nanosecond didn't recognize them. A very disorienting moment. Suddenly I wondered aloud, "Jenny, what am I doing here?" After a pause, I gasped, "Why have I chosen to give up my own home? What am I doing here?"

19
WHAT AM I DOING HERE?

LAST WEEK, AS Granddaughter Jenny and I were saying goodbye, I suddenly blurted out, "Jenny, what am I doing here?" At that moment, I felt out of context, in a place foreign, not in reality at all. I looked around, perplexed. "It's as though I live in a place separated by a membrane from the real world. I can move through that membrane, and you can, too, so we can get to each other, but I don't feel any sense of identity here. No context."

I paused. Maybe I should, after all, still be in my own little cottage in Capitola-by-the-Sea where members of the family have been celebrating milestones and collecting sea glass for 20 years. Where we rented a place at Venetian Court, right on the beach, in 1960, way before we bought the cottage in 1996. Where we have our traditions.

She turned off the car, opened the window, and looked up at me. "I know just how you feel, Gran. I feel that way, too. I like my job in Oakland. I like where I'm living, but I wonder if I belong there. I don't feel at home like I do in my own room in Los Altos. Maybe it will just take some time to develop our new contexts. We'll probably relax when the newness wears off." How could she be so wise so young?

"I'll email you tonight," she said. "We'll keep in touch." She patted my hand, we both shrugged. She closed the door, turned the ignition key, and drove slowly away as she waved out the open window, gave a chipper little beep on the horn, and turned out of sight.

Wiping my eyes, I walked back toward my unit, and stopped to talk with a neighbor. I asked how she was doing.

"Oh, I guess I'm fine, but you know, I don't belong here. I belong in my own home, taking care of myself. Here they bring me my meds, bring me my meals, clean the apartment, tell me when I can water the flowers. I shouldn't be here, but my kids think I should, so I am. I'm lucky though, I have the gift of gratitude and I know I could be in a place a lot worse than this. One thing I've learned is that when you don't want to play tug-o-war, you drop the rope."

How timely for me to hear that. Drop the rope.

I walked on, sat on my patio in the sun with my hands in my lap. I missed days gone by. I missed my families. I even missed my mother! Nancy walked by and I asked where she was going. "Over to Commons B to help get ready for the Valentine potluck we're having today. Are you coming?"

"Maybe," I said. "I think I signed up to bring a salad."

After Nancy had walked on, I remembered something I'd recently read by Ying Lee, the younger sister of fellow resident, Lee Hause. Ying Lee's memoir, *From Shanghai to Berkeley*, is about her childhood in China, college life at UC Berkeley and her life as wife, mother, and social activist. After working in Washington, DC, she returned to Berkeley and wondered, "What am I doing?" She said, "I felt unharnessed. I knew that this was normal. I knew from lots of books that people recommended that it's a transition period. That you are going to feel lost and that you are going to feel rootless."

Another description of the way I felt.

I asked myself, when else have you feel bereft and what did you do? I remembered one bleak afternoon in 1972 when I went outside and planted 12 red petunias and got through the day. I recalled Al-Anon advice: when feeling lonely, call a friend or do something for someone. I stood up, walked over to Commons B, and helped arrange cut fruits on trays. Among the women who were chattering and preparing food, I felt better. When a large sheet cake appeared, I asked, "Wow! Who's giving this?"

Yvonne said, "This is from Phyllis and Medori, both of whom had neck surgery last month and yesterday their neck braces were taken off. They got this cake to celebrate." I cracked up. Where else would two women celebrate the removal of their neck braces by buying a giant sheet cake to share with some 50 friends?

I pulled Yvonne aside and said, "There's something I want to tell you," and related my feelings about maybe not belonging here and feeling weepy.

She, a tender soul, blinked her own tears away, touched my arm, and said, "I think you were so focused on the familiar with Jenny that when she was leaving and you didn't recognize the hills, you felt lost for that moment. It's natural to go through that when you move. But I'll tell you something. I'm glad you moved here."

The fog lifted. I guess this is the right place for me after all.

20
GARDENS IN MY LIFE

THIS IS QUOTED from Mabel Barbee Lee's book, *The Gardens In My Life*, (1970):

> I wish I knew how to make old age seem beautiful to you. All I know is what I have observed in others who apparently have found the secret. I have an inkling that it has to do with keeping the mind alive and interested no matter how afflicted the body, and never letting the divine spark of self-confidence die out. I suspect that more than anything else, it is the deepening understanding that often gentles the eyes of the aged and makes them more tolerant and forgiving of human foibles and their weaknesses.
>
> Grace. it seems to me, is a developing virtue, never fully realized. It is a gradual warming of the heart toward others, no matter what the differences may be. It is kindness reaching out, not afraid to touch another, nor to become involved if needed. Above all, it is the desire to help others as well as one's self and to accept with humility what cannot be helped.

The miners of Cripple Creek used to have a saying that gold is not gold until it is refined. It is through the continuous refining of character, I suppose, that scars tend to fade and the quality of charm in old age becomes real.

It has occurred to me that one never plants a tree or a shrub or a fuchsia slip for one's self alone...it is an act of faith in the months or years to come, a part of the continuing flow of life.

21
YOUR FUTURE LIES AHEAD

DO YOU REMEMBER Art Hoppe (1925-2000)? He was a columnist for the San Francisco Chronicle for 40 years. I found one of his articles and will quote it in its entirety because I agree with what he says and like the way he says it.

> Our poor young people – striving, straining, struggling day after day in a stress-filled world. In sympathy, I would like to give them something to look forward to: old age.

> I recently passed 69 with a backward wave of the hand, and I wish to report that these are the richest years. True, I'm blessed. I still have my teeth, my hair, my dear wife, and enough wherewithal to live comfortably--which is precisely the way we more fortunate members of the older generation live.

> For we have what the young people don't even know they're missing: freedom. To a large measure, we can live where we want, wear what we want, go where we want and do what we want without worrying about the permission of our parents, the approval of our bosses or the judgment of our peers.

No longer are we driven by blind ambition, for most of us know we've reached the highest niche in our careers. At first, the realization comes as a shock. What? We won't be the greatest poet, the wealthiest businessman, the most powerful politician? But on reflection, that knowledge induces a warm serenity.

Sexual flirtations are now merely a delightful game and no longer a grim war of conquest. Should a zit appear on the eve of the annual ball, you easily manage to cheerfully go on living. How I shudder to recall how agonizingly crucial it was to smile just so, to walk with precisely the correct swagger, and to know every single word of every single song on the Hit Parade.

But now the affairs you have are both fleeting and verbal. And your dear spouse tolerantly limits the critique to, 'Well, I don't think she (or he) is all that attractive.'

Your mortgage is paid off, and you no longer have to save for your old age. Your family is even more to be treasured--primarily because your children are grown. If they leave a trail of pistachio shells in the living room or don't take out the garbage, who cares? It's their living room and their garbage. And the orthodontists' bills they run up are for their children.

For the first time, you'll enjoy freedom of travel. No longer will you have to wait in lift-lines during Ski Week or queue up at Disneyland in July. Off-season, that's the money-saving, crowd-free ticket.

The ties on that straitjacket of political correctness are loosened in your case. Should you refer to a homemaker as a housewife, even the most militant feminist will ignore your gaffe. After all, you are obviously a totally irredeemable unenlightened mossback.

Best of all, once you've crossed that mystic divide of 65, you can say no. When asked to judge a snail race or care for a neighbor's chihuahua, you can simply say, "No, thank you." If pressed for an explanation, you might add, "I don't want to." It's not that we older folks don't care what others think, it's that we don't care half as much as we used to.

Ah, that I could have been this free in my salad days. It may be true that youth is wasted on the young, but old age, believe me, is not wasted on us elderly.

How deeply rewarding it is, and how deeply thankful for it I am. My only regret is that it's just another phase I'm passing through.

22

THE WORLD AT YOUR DOORSTEP

IF YOU ARE a person who likes the world to come to your doorstep, a senior living community might be just right for you.

When I was growing up, salesmen came to the door with their wares. Do you recall the Fuller Brush man? The encyclopedia salesman told Mother, "If you love your children, you'll buy these books for them." Someone knocked and even before we opened the door, a woman's voice sang out, "Avon calling!" I liked best the man who came to sharpen knives and scissors.

I remember the grocer, Mr. Stevens, in my hometown of Coquille, Oregon. In the 1930s and 40s, Mother telephoned her order to him. Mr. Stevens put everything into a box, and after school Jack Stevens brought the groceries around to the back door of our house, right into the kitchen, where he carefully placed the box on the counter next to the sink.

When I was in high school, Jack sat behind me because we were seated alphabetically. I liked him and on the days I knew he was delivering, I'd hang around the kitchen or in the yard near the back door. He asked me to go to the Junior Prom, brought me a gardenia corsage, and afterward, delivered me home, to the front porch, and shook my hand as he said goodnight. All that I then knew about romance was from the movies and I had never seen a handshake goodnight.

Well, so much for Jack Stevens.

At the University of Oregon, I met Jim Love, whose father was a grocer in Everett, Washington. Jim had delivered groceries during his high school years. What was it about grocery store boys that attracted me! During the years our four sons were preschoolers, Charlie, our milkman with Berkeley Farms, came in the back door, stepped carefully across the littered kitchen floor, and opened the refrigerator. He checked the milk, butter, and ice cream supplies and stocked us up for the next few days. I didn't even have to think about it unless we wanted cottage cheese. If we did, I'd put a little sign in the window so Charlie would know to bring it in with him.

The diapers were collected, laundered, and returned. Jim dropped a bag of his white shirts onto the front porch and a few days later they were returned washed, ironed, and folded into a neat paper parcel, tied with a string, the amount of starch in the collars exactly as he liked.

As time moved on, most of those services disappeared, but our mail is still delivered. Members of the Farm Food Co-ops receive seasonal produce delivery and I understand we can order online from Safeway, but I've never done that.

Some of you know that what I have done is move into a senior living community. I am impressed with all the conveniences here! Practically at our doorstep, right here on campus, we have book clubs, yoga and exercise classes, Chi Gong, craft classes, and memory classes. Board games and bridge games, lectures, discussion groups, concerts, sing-alongs, and Saturday night movies. The shared laundry is a skip from my door, a copy machine is available, and for a small fee, we have paper shredding services. Prepared meals are available and delivered to our door if we ask. If Anne is inclined to forget to take her meds, someone shows up at her front door with them. Landscape maintenance crews arrive, a cleaning lady comes; so does a massage therapist when I schedule her. We can get our hair cut ($15, ladies), our toenails cut, a manicure. Without even going out the gate. There are parties every few weeks, potlucks and barbecues and birthday cakes, a really good library of 1,000 books. Most of these activities are managed by the residents; the exercise and yoga classes are led by a paid instructor.

Sometimes I feel as though I'm living in a resort. I, who have always liked the world to come to my door, am content in this senior living community.

But something else is more important than all the services and programs. As I've said before, it's the people. The people who live here and those who work here. The staff members are devoted and cheerful. The residents are here for various reasons, mostly something to do with deterioration. Most seem to be good sports, courageous. With grace and concern, they observe the physical decline among us. We are here for each other. We are that important portion of the world who appear on each other's doorsteps.

23
THE OTHER ROOM

" HULLO! I'M HOME!" I announced each afternoon after school.

"I'm in the other room." Mother called out.

"WHAT other room?"

"In here!"

In a five-bedroom house for a six-member family, it was a game to find her. But by following the sound of Mother's voice, my brothers and I could track her down.

Now, 75 years later, I live in a space where indeed I can say, "in the other room." That's it. Two rooms. One is kitchen-office-dining-living room. In Architectural Digest, it'd be called the Great Room, but not here. Both rooms--the other room, the bedroom, plus, of course, the bathroom – total 540 square feet. Easy to find a person or a possession. Simplifies life. Gives more time to be outside.

And outside is where I like to be. With the coming of spring, I am pulled to the far back corner of this campus where seven garden spaces are located, similar to a community garden. A few weeks ago, while the soil was moist after a pretty good rain, I weeded one plot, found a bamboo teepee frame, settled it in the center of the plot, and tied bright ribbon streamers on top. I had seeds from my garden in Capitola, so planted sweet peas around the base of the teepee, scattered marigolds, black hollyhocks, red poppies, bachelor buttons, and emptied some baggies of un-named seeds. We'll see what happens.

Elizabeth came by as I was patting the soil over the seeds and she bent to pull weeds from her neglected strawberry patch. We talked about how lovely the garden area could be. It had potential, but everywhere lay scattered heaps of plastic pots, shards of terra cotta pots, tangled tomato frames, rotten wooden planters, odds and ends. The weedy grass was almost hip-high. We dreamed of a picnic table, visualized pathways of tanbark, chuckled at the idea of painted chairs where we could sit in a row to watch our gardens grow.

Then miracles happened. The maintenance crew mowed the weeds! Next day, students from Cardinal Newman High School showed up. It was their community service day. Three volunteered to weed the unclaimed garden patches. They did a thorough job, smoothed the soil with their bare hands, and swept the walkways. I found a partial bag of potting soil and one of the boys poured it into one of the beds. They stacked the tools neatly and disappeared.

I collected all the plastic pots into a large wheeled cart. Elizabeth and I arranged the clay pots along a rustic potting bench beneath a huge old oak and we agreed that if residents don't show up to claim gardens, she and I will plant nasturtiums.

Looking for ideas, I searched my bookshelves for the Sunset Garden Book. Not there. Oh, that's right. I lent it to someone, but couldn't remember who. On the bulletin board, I posted a notice asking that it be returned. The sign stayed up for almost a week and I began to understand: I had forgotten to whom I had lent it and someone had forgotten that she had borrowed it. Ann Next-door and I laughed about the complexities of living among unreliable memories. Then Nancy said to me, "I have a Sunset Garden Book I never use. I'll give it to you." Within five minutes she brought it, saying, "Now, for certain, yours will show up."

She was right! I came in the door and there on my desk was the Sunset Garden Book and a note saying, "Thanks for this. Now the garden will be ready for my daughter's wedding. (signed) Susan, the nurse." She hadn't forgotten.

What to do with TWO copies? I took Nancy's with me to the front desk to see if I could find Susan and there she was in the lobby! I told her the story. She apologized for keeping the book so long and eagerly accepted Nancy's. So Nancy has enviable empty inches in her bookcase, Susan has a copy all for herself, and I have my annotated copy.

And that's what can happen when you live in this and the other room, and spend more time outside.

24

PEEL OFF THE CALLUS

" THERE IS A feeling part of us that does not grow old at all. If we could peel off the callus, and wanted to, there we would be, untouched by time, unwithered, vulnerable, afflicted and volatile and blind to consequence, a set of twitches beyond control."

That quote from Wallace Stegner's *The Spectator Bird* (1976) seems to explain some of my feelings these days. I catch a fragrance of jasmine and before I realize why, I am suddenly sitting in the sun by the pool on Occidental Avenue in San Mateo Park, where I bought a smaller house after the boys had gone off to school and their father had left. It was the only house with a pool I ever owned. Grandchildren learned to swim there. Sometimes in the dark of night, I'd strip off my pajamas and float naked beneath the moon. Jasmine bloomed along the back fence.

In those years, I was vulnerable. Stumbling and lurching and growing toward middle age essentially on my own. Having a good time. Making mistakes, knowing they were mine. Maybe at the top of my game. Enthusiastic about possibilities.

I thought of this time in my life as recently as April when Joanie and I went to Cuba for eight days and were instructed, "Bring your heart to Cuba." We met people who are enthusiastic about possibilities, about the changes that are taking place in their country since President Obama lifted the embargo.

Two generations of Cubans have grown up with Communism, a consequence to exploitation of their land and people. Some problems have been solved, but the government has been restrictive for 50 years. Now the rules, the laws, are relaxing and we saw the Cubans' enthusiasm for possibilities.

My favorite experience in Havana might be our visit with seniors in a day-care community center provided by the Catholic church next door. The people, mostly women, were clean, well-dressed, eager to greet us, and to play dominoes. I had brought 70 nine-inch balloons as gifts. We blew them up, tied the knot with ribbon and gave them away. As eager as children, everyone gathered around and waited for a balloon, some pointing to a favorite color. One woman, sitting nearby, hid her balloon beneath her dress, between her legs, and asked for another. She wasn't very clever at concealment and everyone laughed with her. I wrote my name and 1927 on a red balloon and gave it to a woman in a red blouse. She took the marking pen and wrote her name and 1927. We held hands and smiled wordlessly at each other, like kindergarten girls who have become friends. She and I, at that moment, were "untouched by time, unwithered, vulnerable."

Here, recently when a fellow resident made a sharp remark to me, I thought about "a feeling part of us that does not grow old" because I felt like I had in grade school when someone taunted me. Quick, in a flash, the feeling welled up. I turned, walked into my safe little Rabbit Hutch, and slammed the door. Shut her out. Stamped my foot. Then took a breath and reminded myself that she is afflicted and blind to the consequence of her remark. I chanted the Serenity Prayer and felt the hurt dissipate. I am not completely "untouched by time, unwithered, vulnerable."

25
AH, MUSIC AND MEMORIES

I have rewarded myself, given myself a gift. Splurged. The reward is for having moved a year ago, as an experiment, to a community for the elderly, and for having made it work for me. I have wanted a Bose radio for about 10 years and now I have one! It sits atop the five-foot refrigerator, just right, its clever cord acting as an antenna. I turn it on by placing my hand gently on the top, like a light touch to the cheek of a loved one. It plays a CD so I've collected all the music brought home over the years from Road Scholar trips. Alaska's Hobo Jim isn't much different from Lee Knight's music from The Appalachians, nor from the Canaller's Songs of the Erie Canal. Circus Music from Baraboo, Wisconsin, Songs of the Underground Railroad from Ripley, Ohio, Sounds of Nova Scotia, and a CD recorded in West Clare, Ireland, bring back vivid memories. None, though, as powerful as that of Emilio Morales who played piano with his five-man musical group in Havana, Cuba, only last month.

Joanie and I noted that in the parts of Cuba we visited for eight days, live music was everywhere! On the streets, in the hotel lobbies, restaurants and bars, at the hotel swimming pool, and in a shopping mall. Usually the groups were five middle-aged men, wearing brimmed hats, looking reserved while playing their hearts out on string and rhythm instruments, and sometimes on a keyboard. Once a saxophone that reminded me of Kenny G. Always singing.

Songs of survival in difficult times, songs of loss, songs of joy and passion, songs of pride and love for their country.

I expected Cuban music to resemble Mexican music, but it differs in many ways. Mexican mariachi music harkens back to rhythms that came with the Germans to (now) Texas in the 1830s. Although music in Cuba is a fusion of Irish, Scottish, English, French, Spanish, and African, we recognized a predominance of African influences. When Africans were shipped as slaves to Cuba in the 16th Century, they were deemed "black tools" and could bring nothing from home. With just their memories and music, they nurtured their culture. Today, so many years later, we hear the call and response of African music, listen to the rhythms of chanting and drums. Estimates are that 60% of current Cuban population is related to the million slaves imported to work the sugar cane fields.

Joanie and I, with the 13 others in our Road Scholar group, were entranced as local musicians played and dancers danced for us and with us. From wild foot-stomping dances to sedate danzón, we were invited to participate. Danzón was my personal favorite; quite formal, proper, precise, complete with men who wore their hats, and women, in dresses with the hemline below their knees, who carried fans. We were told that in earlier days, a secret system developed so a girl, by running her fingers across the top of her folded fan, could let her escort know she liked him. Another motion warned that the dueña (chaperone) was watching. We didn't employ the fan but enjoyed the decorous dancing to exciting music.

So, here I sit, listening to Cuban music on the Bose radio and relishing memories.

26
IT'S A PROJECT

I CAN HARDLY turn my head this way or that. Ouch! Maybe I shouldn't have dragged that 12-foot ladder to a different place. It had to be moved because I wanted to collect the five trash bins scattered around and arrange them out of sight. The ladder is now out of the way, tilted against a shed, and the trash bins are lined up along the backside of the fence. All neat and tidy and satisfying. Very Virgo.

My neck and shoulders will heal and next time I'll be more judicial about what I struggle to move. Be more patient. Ask for help. I'm 87. Lesson learned.

I wish you could see The Gardens! You may remember that I have written of fellow-resident Elizabeth and our dream of an improved community garden area in the back corner of the property. Since a crew of Cardinal Newman High School students removed the weeds and smoothed the soil, six of the seven garden plots are planted. Zinnias, strawberries, nasturtiums, hollyhocks, and spinach. Betsy's artichokes, kale, parsley, iris, poppies, and lettuces look like a Rousseau exotic thicket. The sweet peas I planted are up and blooming, pink and purple. Dorothy's new squash plants are edging over the lip of her plot. Elizabeth has added a salvia, Dusty Miller, a pumpkin vine, and a rescued poinsettia plant.

Along the boundary fence and in the 'grassy' area, we raked up the debris and had it hauled away. I picked up the plastic pots that were lying about and wanted to recycle them, but Betsy worried, "When we are older and no longer strong enough to lift terra cotta pots, we'll have to rely on the lighter plastic ones, so please save them." I collected, sorted, and stacked them out of sight in a back corner. I bet there are 100s of them! All sizes.

Betsy's is part of community thinking. I was thinking only of getting rid of excess. She was thinking not only of herself, but of others. Another lesson learned.

Within the 25 x 15-foot area, we designated "The Picnic Place." Son Sam and his wife Sandra removed a scrawny little tree and its rotten planter box and then reconstructed a neglected potting bench. Elizabeth liked the new redwood counter so much, she found a shallow dish, turned it upside-down to use as a pillow, settled herself on the counter and, while gazing up through the overhanging oak tree, fell asleep.

After the ground was raked and leveled, we set a redwood table in the center and I spray-painted five folding chairs in zinnia colors. Kay, a nearby resident, told me that when she looks out her window each morning, she expects to see a camp counselor setting up for crafts class.

Have you ever heard of carpeting garden walkways? It is the epitome of recycling! The old carpet still deterred weeds, but was unraveling along the edges, so Elizabeth, concerned about trip-hazards, ripped up the old carpet. I waylaid some carpet that was being removed from #27, and Miguel, our very apt maintenance man, cut and lay down new used carpet. Quite grand. Like a hotel hallway. Eventually, we'll add a layer of mulch or decomposed granite. Or something.

Yesterday at sunset, I walked up to The Gardens, sat in a bright orange chair in The Picnic Place and looked around. It felt complete. If my brother John were still alive, I'd tell him that after all these 80 years, I'm still doing what he and I did when we were children. I am making the house complete.

I scanned The Gardens and thought of a day in March, only about three months ago, when Sam, Sandra, and a friend walked back there with me to plan. As Sam and I visualized The Picnic Place, our friend called, "I think over here would be a better picnic place." Sam and I continued talking. She called again, "I don't know why you don't…"

Sam looked up, grinned, and said, "It's a project. It's Mom's project."

27

NOT PERFECT

" TAKE WHAT YOU like and leave the rest." The phrase learned in Al-Anon applies to living in a senior residence. It's not perfect here.

A resident advised, "Get used to it." Well, maybe.

I have objections, none of which is really significant, but each itches until I want to scratch and scream. Then I remember that I have never been a very good rule follower. As an adolescent, I rebelled so loudly that in 1944, I was sent away to boarding school in Portland.

In 2001, when I was 74, a counselor suggested that I take the rebellious teenager still in me and transform her into a self-governing queen. He advised that I keep the sense of independence and add tact, grace, and compassion. I liked that image. It felt wise.

I had thought I had done all right until I moved into this senior community. New challenges. The residents are thinkers; feisty, courageous, determined. Still, a certain amount of compliance is expected. Which rules and routines will I follow without losing my self?

A Mother Goose rhyme from 1695 says, "For every ailment under the sun, there's a remedy, or there is none. If there be one, try to find it; if there be none, never mind it."

Before going to bed, I walk out the door of my little Rabbit Hutch, stand barefooted in my pajamas in the moonlight and evoke the Serenity Prayer:

"God, grant me the serenity to accept the things I cannot change, the courage to change the things I can, and the wisdom to know the difference."

Onward.

28

SOUVENIRS OF MY LIFE

I'VE BEEN AWAY for several days...back in Capitola with son Matt and his wife Joan and their daughter Jamie, then to Los Altos to stay overnight with son John and his wife Holly. Last year, when I leased my little beach house, I cleared everything out of the house and some things out of the garden. This past week, in preparing to sell the house, Matt and I "depersonalized" the garden and filled up the back of my Ford Escape with cobwebby, rusty, dusty, sentimental treasures.

"Mom, do you want these old croquet balls? What about the bowling ball that Jamie painted? I see you still have the old andirons here on either side of the walk."

After Matt and I had finished, had banged shut the tailgate, and Matt had driven back home, I met a friend for lunch and asked her if she wanted any garden decor. She straightened up and said, "Yes! I belong to a garden club and we share decorations." She took the top layer. That afternoon when I drove to Matt and Joan's, I said to her, "Come see what's up for grabs."

"Ooooh, yes, the green watering-can!" she reached into the car. "And how about the bird house? And the yellow bench, these pots, and that galvanized tub." Good, gone. Matt wanted the potting soil, poured it into the tub, and patted it down until it fit just right. Jamie carried the painted bowling ball to their back garden. Reminded me of the first time she played soccer. She was five. The ball was kicked toward her, she bent to scoop it up, and scampered over to the sidelines to show her dad.

By the time I drove over to Los Altos to John and Holly's, I could see some spaces in the back of the car, but invited Holly for a view. She liked the piquet assiette stepping stone, and chose a galvanized bucket "to carry when I pull weeds," and the other galvanized tub. "Could it hold a fire?" she asked. "Oh, the andirons. John will like these...from his childhood on Brewer Drive."

As Holly was deciding where to place the stepping stone, I looked around their yard. Back by the hydrangeas stood a small statue of a graceful woman. A pair of glazed celadon pedestals balanced on either side of the French doors, a yellow watering-can sat by a faucet.

"Holly!" I took her arm. "I'm going to forget decluttering and downsizing! People moving to senior residences have had to divest themselves of things they have loved. They have given away to charities and to strangers. These odds and ends that I used to own are here in your garden now and so am I. To recognize them makes me feel warm and comforted. Like looking through a scrapbook. I like seeing these oddments repurposed according to your and John's style. I like seeing the watering-cans and little benches at Matt and Joan's. I'm glad that Grandmother's bench sits under an oak tree at (son) Sam and Sandra's."

Familiar former possessions remind me of moments in my life. I remember how the clay circle of friends came up from Mexico. It took a couple and their van to haul the piece to Bodega Bay, then my going over with Sam and Sandra to pick it up, and then into my car to take it to Capitola. And now there they are, dancing among John and Holly's roses.

Who cares if the embellishments are a bit dusty, if the buckets are a bit dented? They are souvenirs of my life. I can visit my families and touch my past. I didn't downsize, I just moved those relics to other gardens.

29
THE CASE OF A DISAPPEARING BRAIN

THURSDAY, AS I was walking from a meeting back to my Rabbit Hutch, I stopped to talk with her. She was standing on her patch of patio in the sunshine. Small, neat, her blue shirt buttoned and tucked into her slacks, her hair brushed back. Just standing there with a little smile, enjoying the warmth.

"Hi!" I said. "What's going on in your life?"

She jutted her head forward and stuck out her tongue at me.

I laughed and she did, too. "Bad day?" I asked.

"They're going to put me back."

"Back where?"

"Back in Assisted Living."

I was stunned. "WHY? What have you done?"

"Well," she shrugged. "Last week I made dinner twice in one evening. Then the other day I called my doctor to make an appointment and 20 minutes later, I called again to make the same appointment. The receptionist thought it was funny. I thought it was scary and I told someone here. Maybe the woman who brings my meds. I forget who. So now they're putting me back. I was in Assisted Living when I first came here and then they let me have my own apartment. But, you know, my brain is disappearing. I might forget something important. Maybe they think I'll become a danger to myself and others." She sat down and folded her hands in her lap. "I don't know."

I don't know either. The administration is not careless when making these decisions. Now she must reduce her quarters and augment her services. She'll have a spacious room and private bathroom. She'll take her lounge chair and her TV and her computer. She'll have room for her blue desk and family photos. All her meals will be provided at the communal dining table. Someone will do her laundry. Someone will walk with her as she does her four-times-around-the-ring-road.

This is the woman who only a few weeks ago told me, "You know, I don't belong here. I should be in my own home, taking care of myself, but my kids think this is the best place for me so I am here."

I searched for something encouraging to say and asked, "Have you met Leslee Bond? She's in Assisted Living. The little lady with a big smile and orange-red hair? She's my bridge teacher. She's nine years older than you. Ninety-nine and a cracker-jack. You'll get to live there near Leslee."

"Oh, good," she brightened. "We can play cards. You thought of just the right thing to tell me."

For a moment, she was quiet, sitting in the sun, her eyes closed. Then she smiled in a resigned way and said, "I think I've told you that I have the gift of gratitude. This is a nice safe place. I like it here, but I hate having to go to Assisted Living. But then I know the staff there and I like them. They'll keep me safe and sanitary." She chuckled, "and we all know that's fundamental."

I swallowed my sorrow for her, silently acknowledged fear of my own future, and said, "I'll come over and we can walk together. When will you move?"

"Oh, don't ask me details. You know my brain can't handle details."

30
'TIL DEATH US DO PART

AT BREAKFAST YESTERDAY, Lee said, "I love visiting Europe. The countries are so small, it's like going to a department store. You can be in the shoe department and with no trouble at all, wander into the handbag section, which is right next to perfume. Europe is like that."

I enjoy Lee's perspective. She smiles broadly, treads lightly, and has iron in her soul. I said, "I have a question for you, but you don't have to answer." She nodded. "What's it like to live in a senior community with a husband who has a debilitating condition? I have noticed that among the couples living here, several of the men depend upon their wives for care and attention. How do you live with someone you love and watch him slowly disappear?"

She answered, "Oh, it's not easy. It's so hard for John to manage. You know, he was an economist, a professor of economics. He was brilliant and full of fun. Now he's lost that." She paused and smiled, "He drops things and doesn't notice. He's become a litterbug."

Lee continued, "When the children were dependent upon us and we thought the diaper stage would never end, we could carry on because the children were always making progress. They learned to eat Cheerios, to use the bathroom, to not drop things. My husband will not be getting better. He is still sweet, but his state of being is depressing for him and tiring for me."

I thought about the last years of my father's life. For 34 months Mother managed the LVNs who managed Pop's declining health. She wept with exhaustion and said, "There is only one way out of this. We both understand that, so when he verbally lashes out at me, I know that he is frustrated and probably afraid. He is losing his power. He feels useless. He is ready to die."

In spite of his 88 years and Parkinson's disease, Pop kept his sense of humor. As he was propelled in his wheelchair to the dinner table one evening, Mother signaled to Pop that he needed to wipe his mouth. He looked around at his visiting family and chuckled, "I'm like Pavlov's dogs. You ring the dinner bell and I salivate."

In the wee hours of a dark morning, the night-time attendant, a college student, looked up from his homework and realized that Pop had stopped breathing. Mother was alone now.

Here I have noticed that couples are gentle with each other. Bob and Evelyn stroll along the paths, arm-in-arm. Martin and Myra sit near each other to read in the shade of the grape arbor. Dorothy chuckled, "My husband is still a good driver, but he gets lost so I have to go with him to tell him where to turn. He used to get angry at me when I did that, but now we are a team, each of us equally important. It's fun. And if he dies before I do, I'll have emotional support from all of you."

Sometimes I am paralyzed with admiration for the particular and infinite souls of the elderly. In wisdom, we accept what is. With humor, we are realistic problem solvers. We seem to follow the suggestion of Alex Haley in Roots, "find the good and support it." Simple as that?

Lee smiles, "Iron in my soul? That's because I take iron pills. It hasn't always been there." She rests her hand on my arm, "It's not very simple to be good."

31

THE GOOD DISHES

AMAZING HOW ONE thing leads to another. Friday I was on an errand in the far reaches of Santa Rosa and as long as I had extra time, decided I'd search for Joann's, a fabric store.

Found it. Parked and walked in to wander around. Spied a pleasing cotton print on sale for only $6/yard. Brought it home, spread it out on the sofa, and wondered how I might use it.

Saturday morning: "I know! I'll line the backs of the dish cupboards."

Easy. After removing the dishes, I cut, folded, and pressed the fabric edges, and thumped the stapler. I laughed at myself when recalling that in the mid-1950s, about 60 years ago, I had wallpapered the backs of the dish cupboards in the house on Kings Lane in San Mateo. At that time, we had four preschool boys, and that day two little neighborhood girls had come over to play. I lined up the children on the kitchen floor and with chalk, drew a line around their bottoms to designate their individual places. Then I gave each a shoe box and a handful of crackers, and climbed up onto the drain-board to measure and cut and paste. I sang nursery rhymes as I sliced away a piece of wallpaper and tossed it over my shoulder. I heard a child scrambling to retrieve it. When I finished the first cupboard and turned around, all the crackers were gone. The boys had used their pieces of paper to decorate the kitchen floor, table legs, and themselves. The girls had folded or rolled their pieces and collected them in their shoe boxes. Gender-linked characteristics? Hunting/exhibiting versus gathering/saving?

They held up their boxes and I doled out raisins and Cheerios. On to the second cupboard.

I think I'd still recognize that brown, white, and aqua wallpaper pattern. Different from the green, gold, orange, peach flowers on a beige background I'd used for the cupboards here in the Rabbit Hutch. Same sense of satisfaction in making the house complete.

But, it wasn't complete! The bright yellow everyday dishes clashed with the new lining's color scheme. What to do? Aaaah, I held up a plate from the "Good Dishes." Royal Copenhagen Faince, a soft paste ware from the 1920-30s. About as old as I am. Orange basket-weave rim with gold edge. Nice. At that moment I wondered out-loud to nobody, "Why am I saving these?" I transferred all the good dishes to the new location. The 14 dinner plates hid the fabric. I don't need 14 dinner plates! How many plates, bowls, cups and saucers do I need? Maybe six. Back into their traditional shelves went most of the good dishes. I boxed the yellow French dishes to give away.

Then I addressed the glasses section. Tossed some souvenirs. And on to the last cupboard.

This morning I had a banana-almond waffle on a good plate and tea from a tea cup on a saucer, not a mug. I felt quite elegant. After the first bite, I got up, went into the bathroom and brushed my hair. Then returned to the table, opened my napkin, and sat up straight.

All because I found a piece of pleasing fabric on sale.

32

RUNNING THE RIVER

RECENTLY I WAS in Capitola, staying with son Matt and his family. While they search for a house to buy, they rent a house a couple of blocks up behind Gayle's, a Mecca sort of bakery and deli; and within walking distance to most of the important places such as the beach, the ice cream shop, Shadowbrook Restaurant, the library, a small park, several coffee bars, and a shopping center. All places familiar from when I lived in Capitola.

My little beach cottage has been on the market for almost three weeks and I understand from the realtor that it's been shown over 100 times without a single written bid. Our high hopes have been dashed and the price lowered. And will probably be lowered again. Maybe even another again! You who have experienced the slow sale of a beloved home know the wrench. A lot of life was lived in that little house.

A long time ago, even before I lived in Capitola, I joined supporters of Northwest Outward Bound for 10 days on the Middle Fork of the Salmon River in Idaho. I was in the lead boat, piloted by an experienced oarsman. We roared down rapids and swirled over the to the eddies at the bottom to wait and watch the four other boats splash their way through and they, too, joined us at the side to sit still and wait until the last boat was safe.

During my recent visit to Capitola, I had meals with friends, a picnic with 12 members of our family, walks, errands, and surprise visits with people who stopped me on the street, or called out their car windows, "Donna! Wait. I'll turn around." Those days felt like the rush of the river. To be corny, I was in the river of my life, the current swift and exciting, fulfilling, and refreshing.

As I drove the three-hours from Capitola back to Santa Rosa, I felt as I had when running the white-water river.

And life among the elderly? This campus, pretty with trees and flowers, populated with gentle aging friends who speak softly and move slowly, is the eddy, the back-water, the safety at the end of the white rapids. It's a peaceful time in which I listen to wispy music of Peruvian panpipes and contemplate life's patterns.

In her book, *Firstlight*, Sue Monk Kidd refers to The Velveteen Rabbit who wants to be real and learns that "by the time you have been loved enough to be Real, most of your hair has been loved off and your eyes drop out and you get loose in the joints and very shabby. But these things don't matter at all because once you are Real, you can't be ugly, except to people who don't understand."

Sue Monk Kidd's mother tells her granddaughter, "My wrinkles mean I am getting old."

Sue says, "growing old can be a wondrous passage. The markings of it don't matter, except to those who don't understand. What matters is becoming 'real.' What matters is loving and being loved for a long, long time."

She says, "Grandma is just getting real."

Hmmm. I'll sit here in the shade of this laden green apple tree and think about that.

33

GOODBYE, GEORGE

WEDNESDAY AFTERNOON, GEORGE M. Houser died. He was 99 years old and for several months had been in the skilled nursing center.

You can Google George. He was a Methodist minister, a pacifist, a civil rights leader, author, the founder of Congress of Racial Equality. He and his wife Jean met in seminary school and have celebrated over 70 years of marriage. They are the leaders of a large, close-knit family, all seemingly musical. Several times since I moved here 16 months ago, members of the Houser family have given recitals. For George's birthday party, a seven-year-old great-grandson played the piano. A granddaughter has sung opera arias for us. A daughter, Marty, has led us in songfests.

Several of the family members were here Wednesday evening. At 7:45, about 60 of us residents gathered near the apple tree in Commons C. We stood in the crisp evening air and sang some of George's favorite songs: "We Shall Overcome," "Swing Low Sweet Chariot," "This Little Light of Mine." A resident, another George, himself confined to a wheelchair, spoke gently, "I'd like to offer a song for George." He repeated his phrase until everyone heard him. "This is one of George's favorites," he said and sang, sweetly, clearly, "Dancing in the Dark."

Soon one of George Houser's daughters appeared and said, "He's coming now," and the hearse attendant slowly pushed a gurney carrying quilt-shrouded George among us and on down the sidewalk to the ring road. Jean and the family, then all of us, trailed behind him, in a scene reminiscent of medieval funeral processions, and sang him home. We stood in silence at the back of the hearse and watched the attendant fold the quilt that resident Charlotte Smith had made for George. At precisely the moment he handed the quilt to Jean, a large V of geese swooped above us and I heard women standing near me suck in their breath. "Oh, look," they whispered.

As the gurney carried George into the back of the hearse and the doors closed, his daughter Marty lifted her arm and waved. We all waved and Marty burst into singing, "Goodbye, George, Goodbye, George, Goodbye George, We hate to see you go." People wiped away tears and smiled to one another.

Someone stepped forward to embrace Jean. Others followed. We hugged Marty and hugged George's granddaughter. We hugged each other and faded into the dusk. A quarter moon hung above the skilled nursing center.

I couldn't help but recall a recent letter received from my brother David. He had sent the obituary of yet another George, whom we have known since we were children. David wrote, "When I run across these accounts of old friends, I get a surge of nostalgia and sadness, but I am coming around to feeling that these stories are of a life well-lived."

George Houser has joined those whose lives were well lived.

34
NOT POPCORN

We, about 30 of us, had a party at The Gardens. Bright flowers, bubbles, popcorn, pretzels, lemonade, water and wine. A charming couple sang while he played guitar. Perfect afternoon weather, sun making shadows beneath the huge old oak tree, and a refreshing little breeze.

The party was to honor the Buildings and Grounds committee as well as a few others, people interested in the various areas of our campus. Some came in their garden hats and pearls. I wore my brightest orange shirt. Elizabeth stood upwind and happily waved her wand of bubbles. Residents chuckled like children and flicked their fingers at the iridescent globes.

I have previously mentioned that several months ago, Elizabeth and I noticed that the space in the back corner that holds seven individual garden plots, a potting bench, and a hot house. It was a mess. Only a couple of the garden plots were planted and tended. Trash and discards everywhere. We saw the potential.

With help, we cleaned it up. We both raked. I spray-painted wooden chairs with bright zinnia colors. Elizabeth created large mobiles out of found objects.

On Monday of this week, we held the party, not only to honor the Buildings and Grounds Committee members, but to celebrate the transformation. Six of the plots are now planted. Even the seventh has one tomato and one squash in it. Last year it had dandelions and feverfew and oxalis. The paths are newly carpeted to discourage weeds and the carpets are hidden by fresh mulch. In the plots bright nasturtiums mix with potatoes, tomatoes, squash, Dorothy's kale, and Betsy's artichoke.

I made popcorn and brought bright orange and yellow table runners, and water. Elizabeth brought pretzels, cookies, ice, and wine. We both brought lemonade. We learned that people prefer pretzels over popcorn. Some shook their heads and said, "Gets stuck in my teeth." Neither did guests drink water; we didn't even open it. We poured about a dozen glasses of lemonade, and four bottles of white wine. Now we know: elders like white wine and pretzels, maybe ginger snaps. Forget popcorn and water. Everyone probably would have enjoyed the slices of watermelon, but I forgot to bring them. The next morning, they were still chilling in the refrigerator, so I took them over to the breakfast table and the platter was clean by 8:15.

Across the party, I saw Betsy, who arranges for musical events here, talking with the guitarist and his wife, my son Sam and daughter-in-law Sandra. Sam grinned when he told me, "We have a gig here in February."

During the afternoon a former board member pulled me aside and said, "My neighbor is tearing out a deck and has some used redwood planks that he will give away. Can you use them?" I answered that son Sam is a contractor and he probably would like to have them. She called today to tell me that she had spoken with Sam and he had said, "I bet Mom will come up with an idea for them."

He's right. I'd like to have a raised garden plot that would be wheelchair accessible. I bet Sam could make it. Elizabeth and I could trundle soil and compost from the supply. I think the Buildings & Grounds people might help us.

35
ANOTHER PARTY!

HOW MANY TIMES in our lives do we have the opportunity to sing Happy Birthday on someone's 100th?

In 2002, my mother, Mildred Taylor Rankin, pushed herself more upright in her bed where she lived at the care center in Florence, Oregon. She tilted her gold paper crown over one eyebrow, smiled, and waved to her family, four generations, squeezed into her room. She proudly showed us a letter of good wishes she had received form the White House. She patted her great-grand babies and asked others about school, about their hobbies, and their interests. She looked at all the candles on the cake and said, "We'd better blow hard before the cake melts. Come on, everyone blow!"

I thought of Mother when Leslee's relatives and friends squeezed into Commons B here to celebrate her 100th birthday. I've referred to Leslee before, so maybe you recall that when she wanted to play bridge, she did something about it. She set up bridge lessons and now two tables meet every Wednesday afternoon. We nibble on salted nuts and chocolates, just as my mother and her friends did when I was in grade school.

In the year 1915, when Leslee was born, Harry "Handcuff" Houdini allowed himself to be buried without a casket in six feet of earth at Santa Ana, California. He scratched his way up and when his hand broke through the surface, he was exhausted and had to be pulled out by assistants. That year the Civic Auditorium in San Francisco was dedicated. George Claude patented the neon tube sign. Raggedy Ann was patented. Babe Ruth made his pitching debut and knocked in his first home run. World War I raged on. Demanding the right to vote, 25,000 women marched in New York City. In Detroit, the Kiwanis Club was founded. The Panama-Pacific International Exposition opened in San Francisco. Leslee chose quite a year to be born.

Think of all the changes that have occurred since she arrived.

Last Sunday, not many of us thought of anything but celebrating Leslee. She sat, backed by 100 bright pink roses and surrounded by well-wishers. Guests hugged her, stood close for photos with her. Members of her family served decorated cupcakes, strawberries, and ice cream on passionate pink paper plates. A woman friend played the accordion and we all sang "Today (While the Blossoms Cling to the Vine)." I was stunned almost to tears. That is the song I ask to be played at the Love Family Gatherings. At our celebration of my 80th, Love sons sang that song and I used all my tissues.

For me, "Today," by John Denver, says it all:

I'll taste your strawberries, I'll drink your sweet wine
A million tomorrows shall all pass away
'Ere I forget all the joy that is mine, today.
I can't be contented with yesterday's glory
I can't live on promises winter to spring
Today is my moment, now is my story
I'll laugh and I'll cry and I'll sing.

36
CHECKING OFF THE LIST

AFTER CAPITOLA COTTAGE had sold, I decided it was time to become more of a citizen of Santa Rosa. First, I would open a local bank account. I asked friends where they banked. A name came up several times so one day I walked into that bank and approached the information counter. The woman there was so busy with another customer, she didn't even have time to look up to make eye-contact with me. I waited almost 15 minutes before wandering to the back of the bank to a teller window.

"Good morning, I'd like to open an account here. What shall I do?"

He looked interrupted and said, "Go up front and stand there. Someone will come help you shortly." I went up front and stood there for about five minutes. Meanwhile the girl at the information counter had been replaced by another young woman.

I walked over to her. "Good morning, I'd like to open an account here. What shall I do?"

She didn't look up. "Well, I have to log in here." I waited for about two minutes and walked out the door.

A few days later, I entered another recommended bank and looked around. A woman jumped up from her desk and strode toward me. "Hello, I'm Lisa. I don't believe we've met. What can I do to help you?" Before she could finish her sentence, a man behind a large desk in the corner, looked up, waved, and called out, "Good morning!"

I told Lisa I wanted to open an account in Santa Rosa. She led me to a chair at her desk, showed me a brochure, and asked what balance I'd like to keep. I told her and she said, "For that balance, you will receive free checks and…"

I didn't listen. I had decided and told her so. She asked questions and typed in answers while I perused the choices of scenic checks. In 10 minutes I'd opened an account and chosen checks and a safe deposit box. Lisa walked across the lobby with me, thanked me, shook my hand, and held the door open.

Yesterday I returned to make a deposit and to stash some papers in the safe deposit box. The young teller noted this was my first deposit since opening the account. He asked, "What made you choose this bank?" I told him about Lisa's and the branch manager's friendliness. "Oh," he said. "I think I've heard this story. I'm glad you are with us."

I've also been choosing doctors and deciding what to do about an insurance agent. Seems as though the insurance agent should be local. I visited one who had been recommended. He was pleasant, professional, and patient with me. I felt so ignorant, but this was the first time I'd bought insurance. The last time any was needed, my then-husband took care of it. In the 19 years since, I'd had to make only a few changes: when we divorced and when I became a landlord. Major life changes, not major insurance changes.

Now I'm no longer a landlord. Not even a homeowner. Now maybe all I need is car insurance and a renter's policy on personal possessions. Someone here told me I could get group renter's insurance at a very affordable rate, so I asked. Then I called the agent who had handled the insurance for all these years and found that his rate was only a couple of dollars more and the coverage was better. I asked him about the advisability of having a local agent. "It doesn't make any difference, Donna," he said. "All companies have a central exchange. But we here in Santa Cruz will take care of you, no matter where you are. You can lose your luggage in Istanbul and we'll cover you."

I paid the nearly-due car premium over the phone. He recommended an umbrella policy.

"Why?"

"In case all hell breaks loose."

Done.

I have a smart young local lawyer, a nice dentist, and a good car mechanic. Still working on the doctors.

37
WHAT DID YOU DO ON SATURDAY?

SOME DAYS ARE almost perfect. Last Saturday was one of them. Instead of lurching out of bed to scramble into my clothes and meet for eight o'clock book-reading, I slept in and dawdled over a "gold mine." Remember those? An egg fried in a circle of toast. Cut the hole with a juice glass, melt butter in the frying pan, lay the bread in the butter, break an egg into the hole. I wiped the crumbs off the edge of the glass and poured in fresh orange juice. Savored every bite and every sip and then licked my upper lip.

At 9:30, Ruth knocked. She came in and we talked about bridge lessons until Nancy knocked. Together we walked out the back gate to the shaded pathway along North Drucker Creek to Brush Creek and congratulated ourselves on 2.6 miles in an hour. We returned home, stopped along the sidewalk to chat with friends and moved aside when Barbara chugged out her door, breathing, "Music!" Ruth remembered that two members of the Santa Rosa Symphony, a pianist and a cellist, were scheduled to play for us. We followed Barbara.

Claude Debussy's "Sonata for Cello and Piano" soared over the spellbound audience of about 25. I looked over at Lynne and saw her smiling serenely, her eyes closed, her head tilted in pleasure. I copied her; shut my eyes. Swoosh! There I was on the little farm the summer I'd finished eighth grade. My parents had given me a horse for graduation and with Ribbons came the small farm! My parents, three brothers, and I moved there as soon as school was out to stay all summer. On my recent perfect Saturday, listening to the concert, I could still feel the gentleness of the air. I lay on the hill above the house and smelled the warm dry grasses, watched birds and tree branches, felt the rough earth beneath my back. Almost every daylight hour that summer, I was outside.

One early dawn, I jiggled my 12-year-old brother John awake. "Shhh. Hurry. Get dressed." He grumbled a little and joined me on the back porch. We took off up the gully behind the house until we'd gained higher ground in the woods and trudged farther than we ever had before. We discovered a rectangular arrangement of stones, probably the foundation of a homesteader's cabin, where we huddled in the misty morning light and listened to the little whispery sounds around us. John muttered, "I'm hungry." From my pocket I retrieved a banana, handed it to him, and continued to sit, to hide my breathing, to squint into the shadows in the woods. I felt sure we were not alone.

In September, our family and Australian sheepdog Bootsie moved back into town. That was the summer my sense of wonder and awe awakened. I realized it 74 years later.

After the Debussy performance, Marion and I enjoyed a couple of loops around the ring road before I returned to my Rabbit Hutch. There, I sat at the table by the window and sorted spoons. My grandmother Sarah's grapefruit spoons, a dozen small old silver coffee spoons I had found in Bermondsey Antique Market in London in 1973, an elegant pearl handled cheese spoon, a sturdy one of pewter that was a gift from my husband for my 23rd birthday. I lined up some I plan to give away. They needed polishing so Nancy and I walked along the pathway toward Oliver's, the market that has everything, including silver polish. And as long as I was there, I bought some raspberries. A treat. Just because.

The day ended with a movie in the library. The same library where that very morning, I'd sat transported by the piano and cello music.

Well, the day was not quite over. After the movie, I walked a few times around the ring road. A walk in the moonlight on a clear October evening.

Was that a perfect day, or what!

38
A SHORT BLOG FROM A SHORT ME

I HAVE FIGURED out another advantage of advanced age! It is beyond reduced admission at the movies, 10% Wednesday discounts at Oliver's Market, and younger people holding open the door.

All my life, I've been among the tall girls, 5' 7 ¾" in stocking feet. Always stood in the back row for group pictures and needed to find slacks marked medium-tall, 32". That has not been easy. The L.L.Bean catalog has them, so I order. Recently I received in the mail a pair of delicious plum colored cords, eagerly opened the package, pulled them on and zipped them up. Ooooh, disappointment! They looked slouchy, baggy around the ankles. I must have made a mistake in ordering. Or they made a mistake in marking.

Yesterday when I went for a routine doctor's appointment, the nurse took my weight and height. Aaaah! I'm over two inches shorter than I used to be, 5' 5 1/2". The average height of American women is 5' 4.6". Maybe now I can wear normal length pants, 30".

On the other hand, the loss might be from my spine, not my legs. I need a second measurement. Do I need to be stretched? I'll ask Cynthia, the Feldenkreis therapist, when we meet on Friday.

In the meanwhile, I'll just fold up a cuff on those plum colored cords.

39

FAIRE GAME

LOTS OF ACTIVITY these past few days. Lots of scurrying about. Saturday, November 21, from 10 until 4, we held the 8th Annual Holiday Faire and Tea. Dorothy and Nancy made dozens of traditional sweet and savory two-inch tall scones. Joanie compiled scrumptious fillings and lined up residents to make ribbon sandwiches. Maureen and Margaret were in the Activities Room sorting through treasures for the Albino Pachyderm Sale. A Baked Goods Table and various local and Guatemalan crafts transformed the library and lobby into a bustling marketplace, and Bev attended to numerous details of organizing the Tea.

It was a happy time. Everyone found a job to do. I heard one physically-limited resident say, "I'll sit here by the door to say goodbye to people as they leave." We residents were doing what we all do best: employing our skills to help others. In this case, a fundraiser for Christmas gifts to the staff and scholarships for students in Guatemala. We raised thousands of dollars in one day.

Last year was my first involvement with this event. When I was told I had to wear a long skirt and white blouse to be a waitress in the tea room, I balked and muttered. Then I realized that the traditions were established, so I drove to the nearest Goodwill store and found a long grey skirt for $4.00. I don't wear white so settled on a pale yellow blouse. With the bib apron a part of the costume and my grey cardigan, very little of the blouse showed. No one seemed to mind. I think it's not so important to focus on what we wear as it is to be sure we act with grace, charm, and helpfulness. And to keep the tea hot, the scones plentiful, and smiles on our faces.

As Maureen and Margaret sorted and priced the contributions for the Albino Pachyderm Sale, I couldn't keep away. When my grandchildren were preschoolers, I asked them, "What is the most beautiful word in the English language?" They would remember what I'd taught them and chant, "S-A-L-E!" Yes, high five!

I wandered among the stacks of stuff that residents had brought. Amazing how much excess can be accumulated in our tiny dwellings. I bought a lovely Chinese dressing-table tray. Not that I have a dressing table, but the glazed tray with hand-painted orange chrysanthemums was irresistible. Maybe I'll use it to serve banana-nut bread I bought from the Baked Goods Table. And maybe next year, in a flash of compulsive cleaning, I'll contribute it back to the SALE.

This morning I saw Midori wearing the red cashmere V-neck sweater I hadn't worn for 10 years. Ann came by to show me a colorful top I'd bought several years ago in Alamos, and never worn. It looks just right on her. I showed Nancy a beautiful Foley maple rolling pin I couldn't resist – not that I bake anymore, but I love the pattern in the maple.

The Faire is over, the tea cups packed away for another year, the furniture pushed back into place, and serenity reigns again.

Lots for which to be thankful. Happy Thanksgiving, everyone!

40

IT'S ALL HERE!

IN THE ART corridor this month is a charming assortment of works contributed by the Sonoma County Hookers. That's right – hookers: men and women who hook rugs. Their art renewed my yearning to own such a rug.

So, when I saw in a catalog a 3' x 4' hooked rug of a decorated Christmas tree, I picked up the phone. A "me-to-me" seasonal gift. Anyway, I don't have space on a horizontal surface for a standing Christmas tree. Last year I lifted my dorky little 3' tree out of its storage basket, plunked it on the dining table and plugged it in. I eat, sort mail, read books, and make lists at that table and the tree crowded me.

The rug arrived three days ago and I needed a channel sewed along the top of the back so I could run a rod through. I don't sew, but Charlotte Down-the-Walk does. She said, "This is too heavy to do on the machine. It'll have to be done by hand." I worried that she'd not do it, but I was wrong. I left it with her, and the next morning about 6:30, she arrived at the front door. "All done," Charlotte announced and declined my offer to pay. Later, I learned that she has a fund for the quilts she makes for residents on special occasions. I didn't pay her; I contributed to the fund.

Next I needed a rod or a stick. Looking around, I found a long ¾" stick that last summer I'd painted green and used to prop up tomatoes. The tomato plants are now black from freezing; they don't need sticks any more. When

Mary, Ruth, and John came over Monday to play bridge, I asked John if he had a saw I could borrow. He not only said yes, he noticed that I have a small collection of old Santas, and said, "Aaaah, you collect Santas! Would you like an antique paper maché Santa that's been in my family since before I was born?"

"Yes, I'd love it, especially knowing it's meant so much to you and your family." When I walked over to get the saw, he reached the Santa from atop his refrigerator and I carried the treasure back to my Rabbit Hutch to stand it among others.

After I'd sawed the stick, I called son Sam and he came with his handy power screw driver and wife/partner Sandra. The rug was up in ten minutes, and we sat down to admire the effect. A fine Christmas tree that takes no horizontal space.

This evening I took clippers over to a blue spruce in the corner of one of the parking lots and cut a few sprigs from the backside of the tree, brought them home, shook the rainwater into the sink, arranged them among the Santas, and added small lights. Poured a glass of white to celebrate.

You can understand that this was a very satisfying project; the help came from fellow residents and attentive family.

Not through yet, I needed a wreath for the door and remembered Marion's talking about a group, Starcross Community, over on the coast, who sells fresh ones. I called them.

Here in this group, help that has nothing to do with Christmas is just a shout away. Vera no longer sees well enough to drive so asked if I would drive her to Sebastopol to see a friend who was dying. Of course I would. But by the next morning, when she was ready to go, he had already gone, so we missed saying goodbye.

In other blogs I've mentioned Ruth and her love of butterflies. She is giving away milkweed seeds so next year we will plant them and the gardens might become a resting place during migration. A sort of Airbnb for monarchs.

When we live in community, help is available from every direction. I don't sew. Charlotte does. Vera doesn't drive. I do. Charleen next door needed soda crackers; I had some to share. Joanie has a symphony ticket and won't be going; another will. Dorothy is blind; Nancy brings her to Marie's, and Bev reads to all eight of us, sighted or not.

A good way to live.

41
"OH, THE WEATHER OUTSIDE..."

THESE EARLY MORNINGS are frosty! White crystals sparkle on roofs, lawns, and benches. I particularly appreciate a warm, snug Rabbit Hutch, the hum of the furnace as comforting as a pet cat's contented purr.

It has not always been thus.

Sunday afternoon, sitting on the sofa, feeling a bit chilly, I turned up the thermostat and returned to reading The Geography of Bliss, one man's search for the happiest countries in the world. By evening, I realized I was really cold and the furnace had not responded. After layering on more clothes, I did as I had been instructed to do when needing a maintenance person to come help: I sent an email to resident-services. But it was Sunday. No one available until Monday morning. I snuggled down in bed to read some more.

Morning came. White frost outdoors. I leapt from bed into a warm shower, then pulled on sweaters, and walked over to breakfast of warm oatmeal and hot tea. I sent a second email to resident-services, with two copies to staff at the front desk, and joined the Eight O'clock Reading Group in Marie's comfortable apartment.

Back at nine, I checked the Hutch thermostat: 60 degrees, so I picked up a scarf and the car keys and drove over to Sebastopol to meet two friends. We sat in a warm restaurant, chatted, ate, and dinked around in the Goodwill

Store. It was three o'clock before I returned home, hung up my coat, and checked the thermostat.

Still sixty degrees. Put the coat on and headed to the front desk. "No, Donna, we didn't receive your email order."

So what will we do now?

"Well, it's nearly four o'clock, time for the staff to go home. Will tomorrow be okay?"

I almost stamped my foot in frustration, but standing behind the reception desk, Soonamai noticed, nodded, and said, "Come with me," as she stalked off across the lobby. She found Miguel, the maintenance magician. He came, lay on the floor in front of the wall-furnace, removed the bottom panel, and jiggled parts. Finally he whacked the furnace with the handle of his screwdriver, and it turned on!

Twenty minutes later, the furnace was off and stayed off. Back to the front desk. Again Soonamai tracked down Miguel. "Still here!" and he spoke with the other maintenance man, Bill. From the supply room, they chose a spare part and they BOTH came. Bill checked the thermostat and called out, "Found the other problem! Low battery."

With the new fuse and two new AAA batteries, the furnace settled down to pumping out heat. Problem solved. I am very happy to have a toasty home. I didn't like being cold.

On some mornings in 1986 on the Great Peace March across the United States, when my mittens froze to the oatmeal spoon, I understood why cultures became sun worshippers.

I am grateful to Alice H. Parker, an African-American teacher born in Morristown, New Jersey. Alice, an honor graduate of Howard University, was tired of the inconvenience of fireplaces heating each room, and designed a central gas-fired furnace with a thermostat. Her patent was granted December 23, 1919; 96 years ago next week.

I can't imagine how miserable it must be to have no home, to struggle to sleep with nothing but cardboard and newspapers as protection. On the Peace March we had snuggly sleeping bags and warm jackets, wool socks, knitted caps, so even though we were always outdoors, we were fine.

With new appreciation for warm homes, I'll spend Christmas with sons and their families and others who are members of our extended family. As you hang your stockings by the chimney with care, or whatever you do to celebrate this time of year, I send you all my very best wishes for a cozy holiday.

42

LIFE IN BOTH LANES

OVER LUNCH RECENTLY, I fumbled through an attempt to explain to a 20-something the difference between life in senior years and life at his age. He had asked, "What do you have planned for the rest of the day?"

If I had answered, "Oh, not much," it would have sounded decrepit, so I chirped, "Well, I'll take a walk with a friend and then I'll put away the Christmas decorations and I'm reading a good book, Brooklyn, and I'll walk over to skilled nursing to see Mary. She fell last week."

"Wow!" he brightened. "You have a busy day!" He seemed relieved to think I was living a productive life, that I wasn't yet obsolete.

What if I had said, "I think I'll sit for a while on my little patio in the sunshine. And then I might lie on the sofa to read before I go over to see Mary." That was closer to the truth, so I added, "You know, as we get older, our lives quiet down. We don't so much have the need to do. We strive to be, so instead of living wider, we go deeper. It's a time of contemplation and appreciation. Sometimes I wonder if the old folks we see in their wheelchairs, the ones gazing in a dazed way at nothing, might be living deep rich lives inside themselves."

Having thought this, I was reassured to read in Atul Gawande's book, *Being Mortal*, "We shift as we age toward appreciating everyday pleasures and relationships rather than toward achieving, having, and getting, and since we find this more fulfilling, why do we take so long to do it? Why do we wait until we're old? The common view is that these lessons are hard to learn. Living is a kind of skill. The calm and wisdom of old age are achieved over time."

That is not to recommend that we give up achievements. I believe that the habit of achieving is worth developing. In our family, we have three still in college; three girls, cousins. They earn good grades, are involved in student activities; one participates in dance and one in music, and one is a political activist. They were achievers in high school and I am confident that they will live their lives as responsible, involved citizens. They might even become Giraffes.

Are you familiar with the Giraffe Heroes Project? It was started in the 1980s by Ann Medlock and John Graham who found unknown heroes, commended them as Giraffes, and have put their stories on radio, television, in print, and on the internet. Giraffe stories show the public that headway is being made on the problems of the world, that there are individuals who have solutions and the courage to move into action. The stories feed people's souls, inform their attitudes, and get them moving on public problems that matter to them. The heroes are called Giraffes because they stick their necks out for the common good.

Giraffes are achievers. Elders are achievers, too, in their own individual ways. I encourage you to keep your eyes open for Giraffes and for opportunities to become one. Let Ann Medlock know. I was a Giraffe once.

43

TELL ME A STORY

LAST WEEK, ONE of our residents died as a result of a car accident. One of her daughters came here, and when she visited our reading group, we listened as she spoke of her grief, the details that needed attention, and her feelings when reading her mother's journals. "I am finding out things I didn't know about my mother. She wrote about her life and her concerns. As I sit reading her stories, I feel her presence. She is close by."

Rachel Naomi Remen, MD, in her book, *Kitchen Table Wisdom*, says, "I live in a world of stories. We cannot replicate stories because our lives are unique. Our uniqueness is what gives us value and meaning. Yet in the telling of stories, we also learn what makes us similar, what connects us all, what helps us transcend the isolation that separates us from each other and from ourselves." She continues, "Stories are the language of community. The real epidemic in our culture is not just physical heart disease; it's emotional and spiritual heart disease: the sense of loneliness, isolation, and alienation that is so prevalent in our culture. In my work, I often find that there is a great hunger for a sense of connection and community. Community is a place safe enough for people to talk about what is really going on in their lives, to tell their stories."

In a few days I will lead a memoir-writing workshop for a dozen or so adults. I'll share with them my enthusiasm for writing our stories. I believe that our need for storytelling is basic. It is a way to figure out who we used to be and how we got to be who we are now. It heightens awareness and increases our appreciation and humor, our sense of relatedness and continuity. We discover the important themes and patterns of our lives. Writing is cathartic. Someone once told me, "When you are through demonizing your mother, you can get down to the real story-telling."

A friend sent a New York Times article that said studies show that children benefit from learning what their ancestors faced. "There is a direct correlation between knowing family stories and self-confidence. Children are more resilient, less traumatized. They have a sense of being a part of a larger family."

In 2007 I published a collection of short stories that comprised a memoir and gave the book to members of my family. A nephew wrote, "I am so thankful you saved these stories for our family. My girls ask me about Grandmother and about my dad. Now I have these stories to read to them. It is important to me that they know where they come from."

A note I recently received said,

> "Every life is heroic and yours is no exception.
> With gratitude from the bleachers,
> (signed) The Universe"

I like that. Every life IS heroic and deserves to be recorded, read, and remembered.

When we write our stories, we give ourselves and our loved ones gifts that only we can give. When we are aged and are living in senior communities we have time to write our stories. In the years to come our descendants will read our stories and feel close to us.

44

CHANGES

IN THESE SPACIOUS days, I sit in my Rabbit Hutch at the table by the window to have a cup of tea and a toasted tuna sandwich. And I gaze out at the misty rain. It's shortly after one o'clock in the afternoon and the empty walkways are glistening. I think many residents nap at this time of day.

Oh, there's a neighbor, her arms tightly folded across her chest, standing outside her front door, sheltered by the overhanging roof, looking to her left and to her right. I see her often, stepping outside to peer around and then maybe walk down the pathway and back again, looking, looking. I think she is lonely. And she must feel fearful as she knows she has dementia. She has been a bright woman with career responsibilities and world-wide travel adventures. She can remember to speak to some of the staff in Spanish but can't remember to get a spoon for her oatmeal. She shivers. Her fear is as cold as creek water.

Last week, another resident smiled up at me from her motorized wheelchair, "You know, we experience significant diminishments and keep right on." She's a woman who, 75 years ago during World War II, joined the Navy so her father could put a star in the window.

One thing about living in a senior community, the changes are frequently not ones we'd call good. But they are inevitable. We grow to know the privilege of being alive. We learn to face reality.

I remember a realistic Chesapeake Bay soft-crab boatman whose colorful philosophical phrases tickle me. He talked about his work. "I'm like a barnacle and I'll stay stuck to this business 'til they pry me off." He noted a change. "I can't see as good as I used to. Now my boy, he can see a gnat on the moon." He summarized. "Too many changes. Ever'thins turnin' on us. How can you have family time when they're all scattered like corn. Our yonguns? Today if they lost their can openers, they couldn't survive. Now my wife, she had a stroke, but she's okay. She's got her re-memory back."

I'm working on keeping my re-memory.

Stephen Hawking, who developed his simple, elegant theory of time and space, advises other disabled people to concentrate on things their disability doesn't prevent them from doing well. He says, "Don't regret the things it interferes with. Don't be disabled in spirit as well as physically."

When asked how he felt about being confined to a wheelchair, he answered, "Thank you for asking. It's temporary, of course." He knows about changes.

I like the humor of a 27-year-old who left a comfortable job to attend graduate school. I asked her about the changes this move would entail. "Well," she said, "after you've had a doorman, it's hard to go back to not having one." She laughed and shrugged. She knows about changes, too.

In a discussion group called Transitions, our leader suggests we develop a high tolerance for ambiguity. She asks, "How do you sustain yourself during the changes of aging? How do you keep a sense of safety, a sense of being grounded in the face of the changes regarding the planned expansion of your facility?"

One member answered, "I can get used to the changes, but what bothers me is my sense of being over-treated and under-informed. That feels insulting. It makes me angry so I can't trust."

Our leader suggests, "Think of this period as an experiment. You're living at the cutting edge. It can be exciting. I mean living as an elder or living as a resident watching fearfully the planned building changes. How can you change that fear?"

In this conversation, I told about the fear I felt years ago when my husband left and I was unprepared to take on the responsibilities of single life. I was immobilized to the point where I wandered around the house muttering, "I'm a child of God. I'm a child of God." Then after about a year, I realized that my fear was contradicting my faith. Fear and faith are inversely proportional. When I practice my faith that anything is possible and things usually turn out okay, my fear dissipates.

I have reminded myself that life is an experiment, and therefore, there are no failures. Sometimes it works and sometimes it doesn't. I think that with the accumulation of years, the ego shrinks. It gets as wrinkled as old hands. When the ego shrivels, we can take risks. We have the freedom to try new things.

Facing the changes of growing old takes courage, resourcefulness, and humor. I would hope that with consciousness and grace, the fears and worries about aging will disappear like breath from a mirror.

45

I'LL HAVE PEPPERMINT

WE RESIDENTS CELEBRATE birthdays. I've written before about how we gather in the library, play a group game, sing songs, tell stories, all to salute everyone who has had a birthday in the past two months. The master of ceremonies wears a silk hat – a birthday cake with candles – and keeps things moving along. The last event on the program is the open mic and those who wish to, come forward to recite a poem, read something, or tell a story. Then we troop down to Commons B for ice cream and cake on tables decorated with pastel cloths and flowers.

Last week Patrick came to the open mic and told us about a friend, a woman, who lives in Montana. She had come into town to do errands and had stopped in an ice cream parlor for a treat. No one was at the counter to serve her. No one was to be seen except a man sitting at a table in the corner with coffee and the newspaper. He lowered the paper to sip his coffee and the woman stared. She was quite certain it was the heartthrob movie actor, Paul Newman. She was flustered and when the manager appeared behind the counter, she had a hard time deciding which ice cream cone she wanted. She kept glancing over her shoulder and was sure it really was Paul Newman. Same intense blue eyes and pleasant expression.

She made every effort to look cool and finally decided on peppermint, fumbled with her wallet, paid, put the change away, and went out to her car.

As she was about to open the car door, she realized she didn't have her ice cream cone, so re-entered the shop, looked on the counter, looked at the server, and looked at Paul Newman.

He smiled and said, "It's in your purse."

46
COUNTING YOUR CHICKENS

SOMETIMES I RUN across a phrase, sentence, or paragraph that I want to share in a blog. Today I have an entire story!

At eight o'clock each weekday morning, six residents meet in Marie's living room to read. Two of us are legally blind, two strain to hear, and one falls asleep almost as the book is opened. I read orally such authors as Deepak Chopra, the Dali Lama, and currently, Robert Reich. Thought provoking books of substance.

The final few minutes of each morning session, we are reading *My Grandfather's Blessings*, a collection of stories of strength, refuge, and belonging by Rachel Naomi Remen, MD. This morning's story was "Counting Your Chickens." Here it is:

> When she was eighty-four and newly widowed, my mother had come from New York City to live with me. Frail and very sick with a heart condition, her physical needs were complex and I had found her care overwhelming. Over and over she had sudden attacks of pulmonary edema, a sort of internal drowning from which I would rescue her by placing rotating tourniquets on her arms and legs and injecting her with morphine. It was clear that time was running out, and I became concerned not only for my mother's physical well-being, but also for

the state of her soul. She was not a religious woman, and what rituals she observed seemed more like superstition than spiritual practice. I had read somewhere about the importance of encouraging old people to reflect on their lives in order to die in peace. Without such remembering it would not be possible to receive and offer forgiveness, to uncover meaning and to complete a life well. I did not know much about such things then, but I believed what I had read and wanted the best for my mother. Yet every attempt I made to encourage her to reflect on her past and her relationships was rebuffed.

Some of my friends were involved in spiritual practices of various sorts, and one by one I had invited them over to talk with her about their spiritual paths. A few even attempted to interest her in their ways. She listened politely to their enthusiastic discussions of such things as tai chi, mindfulness meditation, yoga, and vipassana. But afterward she would tell me that meditation just wasn't for her. It was too quiet.

As she became sicker, I became more intent on my agenda. A non-meditator myself, I even began to sit for fifteen minutes in the morning and invited her to sit with me. Surprisingly, she agreed with enthusiasm, but every time I opened my eyes I would find my mother looking at me with great love. After a few weeks of this, I suggested that we abandon it but she refused, saying that she enjoyed having the chance to look at me for fifteen minutes every morning. Eventually I just gave up.

So I was overjoyed when one evening in the living room after dinner, my mother sighed and spontaneously closed her eyes for more than an hour. Once I had determined she was not asleep, I sat in silence with her all that time. When at last she opened her eyes and looked at me, I asked her what she had been doing. "Why, I was counting my chickens," she said with a smile.

Meeting my puzzled look with a laugh, she told me that it had suddenly occurred to her as she was eating dinner (it was chicken) that she had eaten a chicken once or twice a week for many years. She had begun to calculate this in her mind: two chickens a week, fifty-two weeks a year times eighty-four years turned out to be more than 8,500 chickens. It seemed to her to be a great number of chickens just to keep one old woman alive. She had closed her eyes then to try to imagine what 8,500 chickens might look like. It had taken some time, but she finally had a picture of them in her mind. It had been overwhelming. "All that innocent life," said my mother.

She had begun to wonder whether she had been worth this sacrifice. And so she had begun to review her life, looking at as many of her important relationships as she could remember, examining her own heart and her own motivations. It had taken a long time, but at the end she had realized that while she was certain that she had disappointed and even hurt people in the course of her life, she could not remember deliberately causing pain or harm to anyone, or resenting anyone else's good fortune or hating anyone or taking something that was not hers or even telling a significant lie. She smiled at me again. "I believe I have been worthy of my chickens, Rachel," she said.

I think life has an elegance that far exceeds anything we might devise. Perhaps wisdom lies in knowing when to sit back and wait for it to unfold. Too hasty an activism may lead to lesser outcomes and, more important, may cause us to trust only ourselves rather than learning to trust life.

47

WRITE YOUR OWN OBITUARY

IN LATE FEBRUARY, I finally put together a workshop on Writing Your Own Obituary. I wrote a notice in the Friday newsletter, taped a sign-up sheet onto the table in the lobby, and arranged chairs in Commons B.

I had led a couple of such workshops in Alamos, Sonora, Mexico, where I used to go for a few months each winter, so I cobbled together my notes, checked the New York Times obits, and felt ready. Surely a dozen would sign up.

Twenty-five registered, with 20 the final count around the table. Two forgot, one had said, "I signed up, but probably won't come." One had a conflict, and one developed high blood pressure, and decided to take meds, lie low, and read a book, "or," she said, "I might need an obituary."

After introductory remarks, I gave a prompt, "If you had only four or five lines of ink or minutes of time left, what would you write?" I asked that everyone take a deep breath. "You have three minutes to write. Don't stop. Don't edit. Just write."

I told them that their relatives or whoever is going to write their obituary will be grateful to find one already done...or even partially done. My brother David is ten years younger than I. When our mother died at age 100, he wrote an obituary. When I arrived at their home, David asked me to look over what he had written and add anything I thought pertinent. I added quite a bit. We were stunned to realize that the mother he knew was quite different from the mother I knew. We were as accurate as we could be, but it'd have been much easier if she had written her own obituary.

In the writing workshop, I read some published examples. Most were typical resumes of dates, facts, people's names, and "he died surrounded by his loving and devoted family." We saw few glimpses of the essence of the person.

Then I read a couple of the New York Times obits: "George Smith (name changed), 88, whose career as a painter covered more than 50 years, has died. He was a brilliant conversationalist and loyal friend. He leaves his wife Mary and son Henry."

I think I'd like to have met George.

Another: "Leo Lester. The Colgate Boys of Summer have sadly lost one of their charter members. Leo, keep hitting 'em straight."

Leo is warmly missed in the club house and probably by everyone who knew him.

I asked the people in the class to write two or three sentences about themselves, using third person. It wasn't easy. Then I asked that they each write a summary of their life in six words. That was pretty fun.

I read a long obituary that consisted of the introduction/resume, a paragraph about his family, three paragraphs about his career (pediatrician), and then, finally a paragraph that gave us a picture of him as an individual: "Bill was a lifelong Episcopalian, an ardent family man, a long-time aficionado of thoroughbred horse racing, and a passionate New England Patriots fan from the club's inception. Besides his three children, he is survived by six grandchildren, of whom he was exceedingly proud."

Following a format, the workshop participants wrote rough drafts. The goal was to open up to the possibility of writing an obit as a gift to our family and to increase the chance that our obituaries say what we want them to say. How do we want to be remembered? This is a good opportunity to let our descendants know us.

I knew that resident Rosemary was thinking about our workshop when she told me she'd read an obituary that said, "In lieu of flowers, please promise you will not vote for Donald Trump."

48

OH, HAPPY DAY!

LAST WEEK, ASSISTED Living resident Leslee stopped me in the lobby. She lay her hand on my arm and with an intensely worried look on her bright face, said, "Donna, the pictures hanging on the walls in Assisted Living are terrible. Can you do anything about them?" I looked at this ever-so-slender almost 101-year-old fireball with her painted nails and bright orange hair, and thought how much I love her. She knows the difference between aging and living a long time.

Standing together there in the lobby, I reminded her that I am responsible for the Beauty and Decor Committee and that my main job seems to be hanging pictures. I would figure it out.

The next day, Rosemary pushed her walker along the sidewalk and brightened when she saw me.

"Donna!" she called out. "I have something to ask you. The paintings in Assisted Living are so bad. They are dark, have heavy frames, and are quite depressing. I understand you can do something about them. Would you, please?"

I asked her if she'd been talking with Leslee and she shook her head no. I asked her if she and Leslee could meet me near the art storage closet the next day about mid-morning. Rosemary replied that she could meet at 10:30, but she gets on the bus at 11:30 to go stand with Women in Black down on the corner of College and Mendocino Avenues. Every Friday morning without fail, she joins Women in Black with their peace placards. Rosemary is 93.

Exactly at 10:30, I came along the hallway, and there they were snug in green wing-back chairs, waiting. I brought out a couple of paintings. They approved of one, but rejected the other. I brought out two more. And two more. We collected the ones they liked.

After Leslee returned to her room and Rosemary went to the bus, a resident friend, Nancy, and I loaded the pictures into a laundry cart and wheeled them to Assisted Living. As we began to unload them, to set them on the floor, to lean them along the wall, the Director of Assisted Living hustled toward me, a concerned look on her face. "If you leave those there, someone will trip over them."

"Oh. Where do you suggest?"

"Over there near the piano."

"Okay. It'll probably be a few days before I can be back to get them hung."

"Well," she admonished, "you'd better put in a work order."

"I will," I said and wondered to myself how many days would pass before someone would come to help with this project.

It was almost noon when I finished placing the work order and I was in my apartment, eating a salad and reading a book when the phone rang. It was the Director of Assisted Living and she said, "Miguel is over here ready to hang the pictures. What shall I tell him?"

"Tell him, please, that I am on my way!"

That's the quickest reply to a work request I've seen in the 2 1/4 years I've lived here! It usually takes at least a week for work orders to be honored. I had been prepared for frustration. Now I hurried over to Assisted Living and Miguel who would help me hang the pictures.

"Okay, Miguel, the first one goes right here." While he marked, measured, and hammered, I decided on the placement of the next one, and the next one, and the next one. We were ripping right along when Leslee showed up and I asked her what she thought about the pictures so far. She carefully looked around and said, "I think that one is too low." and "I think that one would be better over here." We made the adjustments and by three o'clock, Miguel had hung 18 pictures.

"You happy, Boss?" he asked.

"I'm happy, Miguel. What about you?" He nodded and grinned, gave a thumbs-up.

"Are you happy, Leslee?"

"I'm happy, too. Here comes Rosemary. Are you happy with the pictures, Rosemary?"

"Yes! This is so much better!"

Everybody happy. Life in the Old Folks Home. Happy.

49
TAKE CARE!

" TAKE CARE OF yourselves!" our mother told us as we bolted out the door and jumped into the car to return to the University. She stood on the porch, waved, pretended she was checking the border flowers as she lowered her eyes to hide her tears, waved again, and called out, "Take care! Take care of yourselves."

I thought of that scene as I listened to the millions of words shouted out during the Republican Convention two weeks ago and in the Democratic Convention last week. Such unabashed demonstrations of people exercising their right to gather and speak out, supporting the candidates they believe will take care of them. Lots of speeches promising to do just that.

And then we heard from President Obama whose greatest one-liner was a throw-away three-word phrase: "Don't boo...VOTE." Not shouted, not demanded; spoken almost as an aside, as a spontaneous thought.

And I whooped with excitement! That's right! We need to take care of ourselves. We each need to vote! It's imperative that everyone votes. That's our democratic way of making an effort to take care of ourselves.

In recent years, since I've moved into this residence for the elderly, I have heard complaints, moans, and whines from people who now, in their impaired states, feel helpless. As though they need someone else to care for them. And, yes, that is true, to some extent. But not to the extent that they might believe.

I think it was 101-year-old Leslee whom I heard demand, "Stop your complaining. Instead, draw up a petition and have everyone sign it. That way you'll have a chance of changing whatever you feel is important. You want different food? Get organized. Get a group. Go tell the cook. See what happens."

When I told a staff member in the front office of a situation I felt helpless to change, she gently reminded me, "You know, you need to take that to Resident Services. That's the office right down this little hall. Let them know. See what happens." I did. Nothing happened.

Another time I complained to a friend here that whenever I drove off campus, I came back to find someone had parked in the space assigned to me. I stormed around in frustration, and she asked, "What are you going to do about it?"

I realized the administration would do nothing about my invaded parking space. I had to take responsibility for myself, so with a red marking pen, I highlighted the sign that said "Resident Parking Only," three times underlining Only. I left a note on the intruder's windshield. It worked! Now when I return, I zip right into my own reserved parking space.

Several years ago I was in Oregon saying goodbye to my youngest brother, David. Our brother John had died some time ago and I've lost track of our other brother. I patted David's chest and looked up at him. "You take good care of yourself, David. I used to have three brothers and now I have one, you."

He grinned and patted my shoulder. "You take good care of yourself, too. I've always had one sister, you."

What is Bernie Sanders saying? He's saying just what Mother said, "Take care of yourselves." Just what Leslee is saying, "Get organized." Just what David is saying, "You are important." Just what President Obama is saying, "Don't boo....Vote."

50
AH, CHANGES

REMEMBER WHEN WE worked at jobs that we didn't particularly like, or where someone in the office was offensive or the principal was egotistical and we waded through those ordinary days until TGIF and the upcoming weekend? We had children at home to feed and to send to the orthodontist. We had spousal duties and social obligations. We lived through decades of doing what was expected of us.

And now? Where I live, in a senior community, we can choose to be dutiful and responsible, or, without guilt, we can choose to sit in the sun and do nothing or sit on the couch and read. Such are some of the rewards of getting old. But, when we look idle, we are still alert. We are appreciating the stillness, the spaciousness, the serenity of our lives. Even with twitches of pain and fallible knees, we gaze affectionately at red zinnias in a neighbor's patch of garden, we share still-warm applesauce, we feel a part of an intimate group and a universal "oneness."

Katrina Kenison, in her book, *The Gift of An Ordinary Day*, says, "I realize there are qualities of mind and heart in me that I am grateful for. I recognize, emerging slowly from beneath the layers, the optimism that has always made me *me*. My faith in other people, the sense of wonder that dawns as fresh in me each day as morning. The idealism that is both my nature and my gift. The creation of a self, it seems, at this late stage of the game, is more a process than a project, more about opening and allowing than forcing and doing."

Living daily, the view back longer than the view forward, reminds me that a simple change in focus can improve the tone of a day. Recently one morning, I wakened and asked once again, "Tell me. Just why am I here?"

I answered, "You are here because you want the experience of living in a community. You chose this place so your children would not have to choose."

"Oh, yes, that's right." So, reminded of why, I recalled the admonition, "Thoughts are things. Choose the good ones." As a proclaimed peace activist, I prod myself to create peace nearby. To start at home. Within myself.

Again, Katrina Kenison, whom I paraphrase, "If we are going to live the life we've dreamed, if this place is to become a home built not just of walls and beams, but of love and peace, then both the dwellings and the people in them will require steady care and attention. Peace, patience, and understanding will have to grow and be nurtured here first, if ever we are to carry peace and compassion out into the world beyond our door."

These days, these ordinary days, life is shifting and I need to welcome the change and shift along with it, hopefully with a light heart. In *Women Who Run With the Wolves*, Clarissa Pinkola Estés says, "Mend the part of the world that is within your reach."

Perhaps it does not have to be such hard work after all.

51
TOAST THE POST

"ABOUT FIVE MONTHS ago, I was browsing through the thick volume named *A Pattern Language* by a group of Berkeley architects including Christopher Alexander, Sara Ishikawa, and Murray Silverstein, published in 1977. These were the architects who influenced the design of my current home.

In describing the arrangement of a living-space for one person, the authors say, "Conceive a house for one person as a place of the utmost simplicity; essentially a one-room cottage or studio, with large and small alcoves around it. When it is most intense, the entire house may be no more than 300 to 400 square feet." (Talk about the current Tiny House movement!) My space is larger, about 540 square feet, with a separate bedroom and bath.

To pay the bills, address letters, and write, I sit at an old table in a single-room combination of kitchen, dining table, seating area for TV, reading, and conversation; storage cupboards, an open pantry, office files, and an alcove for hanging jackets. Each of these areas is in a niche around the perimeter of the room. The book says, "In essence, it is simply a central space, with nooks around it."

In all the 30 years I've had the sofa, it has never been more conducive to napping than it is now, settled in its own niche beneath the windows. The kitchen along the back wall is open, but visually separated by a soffit and a change of flooring. The jackets, an antique chimney cupboard, and the writing table share a niche that formerly was a 12-foot closet. These spaces give a sense of order and rhythm to the room. Sometimes I just stand at the front door and gaze around, feeling satisfaction and contentment.

A Pattern Language also discussed columns. "A free-standing column plays a role in shaping human space. It marks a point. The main function of the column from a human point of view, is to create a space for human activity." I walked over to the lobby where ten columns, along with nooks, define spaces for coffee service, conversation, display of goods for sale, our mailboxes, and public notices. Sighting down the double row, I saw that the columns give perspective to the entire area, as well as creating cozy, human-scale, invitingly intimate niches.

I wanted a column!

So, in June, when I returned to Santa Cruz County to see family and friends, I stopped by Crawford's Antiques to check out their supply of old columns. Son Sam, retired builder, had advised me, "Eight-inch diameter, Mom." I found just the right one, except it was, as Suzy Crawford said, "front porch green," with many layers of blistered paint beneath. She said she'd scrape down until she found a color I might like, then smooth and finish it. I'd be back in August. It would be ready.

It was. And it was/is beautiful! Beautiful to those of us who like old, battered pieces. Beautiful to me who likes the rusty bricky color and a surface smoother than silk. We loaded it into my car.

At the intersection of the open end of the kitchen and the little hallway leading to the bedroom, Sam and his wife Sandra installed the column. A few days later, I invited them back for a glass of wine to celebrate this addition. The column, the pillar, the post "makes the house complete." We lifted our glasses to toast the post.

Every morning as I come into the kitchen to put on the kettle, I pat the post. A good way to start the day.

52

DRIED APPLES

TODAY I AM going to dry apples. I've borrowed a dehydrator from Joanie and will slice apples, three horizontal slices per apple. They rest in a bowl of watered lemon juice before I arrange them on the screens and turn on the dryer for about 36 hours.

First, I need to pick the apples. We have over 100 fruit-bearing trees here. Thirty-five years ago, when this community was in the planning stages, a member of the committee, professor of botany at Sonoma State University, Ken Stocking, declared, "We need 100 fruit trees and 100 rose bushes."

So, these bright autumn days of 2016, any of us can gather apples, oranges, lemons, figs, pears, pomegranates, quince, grapes, and roses. Lots of roses. I'm going to pick 25 apples. I think there's a laden tree over in Cluster C.

Today, the last Sunday in September, is a quiet morning. I will gather apples; core, peel, slice, and dry them. My space here will be as aromatic as the canning kitchen I had when I was a fair-weather farmer living in a sprawling yellow house in an apple orchard near Elkton, Oregon, during the 1990s.

53
GOOD IDEA!

WANT TO KNOW why it's a good idea to move into a senior community?

Because when you have a computer problem, there is someone nearby who can help. For years, to print the blog, I have written it, printed a hard copy, set up the hard copy next to the computer. Then I brought up the blog site and copied – I mean I typed again – from the printed copy, the blog.

This morning Ruth came over to talk about something else and I asked her if she has a MacBook Air like mine. She does. I told her how I have been publishing the blog and she exclaimed, "Oh, can't you just copy it into place?"

"No, I don't know how."

And she showed me. I will now try to follow her directions and see what happens. If it works, it'll save all sorts of time.

And that's a reason it's a good idea to move into a senior community!

54
A DAY WITH RUTH AND NANCY

FRIDAY EVENING, NANCY asked me, "Are we walking tomorrow? Should be a lovely day!" She waited for my answer, her pretty faced lighted by her smile.

"Okay," I agreed. Who could resist Nancy? "I'm playing bridge with Ruth at seven o'clock this evening. I'll ask her if she wants to go." Then I forgot.

Next morning about nine, Ruth called, "I hope we're walking this morning."

"Yes, we are. Nine-thirty, my place."

We three octogenarians have been walking the nearby creek paths on Saturday mornings for over a year now. We start out peppy and after a mile or so, begin to slow down. We have found a bench where we sit in the shade for a little while, wiggling close so we all fit.

We talk about anything that comes to mind. We talked again about how to pare down our stuff. I mentioned a small book called just that, *Stuff*, by Steve Neff, in which he says, "Identify the essential, eliminate the rest." He also stresses (in heavy print), "Don't leave it for the kids!"

Nancy suggested that treasured family photos be put on an e-device that shows the pictures in rotation, a few seconds at a time. Her daughter reduced several scrap-books this way and Nancy sees the photos every day. Another idea is to have a bonfire and everyone tosses pictures of relatives no one knows. One friend suggests we discard pictures of people three generations ago. The other pipes up, "Those are our ancestors!"

Each time I visit friends and family for a few days, I take a fat scrapbook with me for their perusal. One of these days, I'm going to start tossing those books. But not quite yet. They are still on the essentials list; records of important parts of my life.

Ruth is going to include old photos of friends in her Christmas cards and share memories of times past.

We walked along, chatting, for an hour or so until we'd circled back toward home.

"Bye. Nice walk. See you at one o'clock,"

"One o'clock? What's then?"

"Remember? We have tickets to the Santa Rosa Symphony rehearsal."

"Oh. Right. See you at one."

Cleaned up, not dressed up, except for Ruth who glowed in a jewel toned silk blouse, we drove to Green Music Center on the Sonoma State University campus. This is the Santa Rosa Symphony's 89th year. Mine, too. I'm celebrating with season tickets for Conductor Bruno Ferrandis' final year here. He says, "For my last full season as Music Director of the Santa Rosa Symphony, I want to remind you who I am through the spirit of programs and artists who are close to my heart." His guest on Saturday was his brother, Jean Ferrandis, an internationally acclaimed flutist. Leonard Bernstein said of him, "(Jean) is Pan himself."

"I wonder if the entire Ferrandis family is musical," I said. "Imagine how proud their parents must be!"

What a treat to sit in Weill Hall, gaze out the windows toward the rolling rural hills, and listen to gorgeous full music, and maybe even doze a little.

Back again, Nancy asked, "Are you going to the movie in the library tonight?"

"I don't know." I answered. "What is it?"

"I forget," she said. And Ruth, who is on the film committee, announced, "It's The Magic Garden. Very touching. British classic. Nice."

"Okay, I'll go. Will you?"

"Yes. Wouldn't miss it. Shall we sit together?"

Of course. Together. The entire day.

55
YOUR IDENTIFICATION, PLEASE

"HAVE YOUR ID and boarding pass ready." An announcement at SFO security. The officer looks at me and says, "You won't have to remove your shoes and jacket." He can see, identify, me as an elder. One of the privileges of being old is not having to take off your shoes when going through airport security.

Phoebe and I have just completed our 14th Road Scholar (Elderhostel) trip together. Phoebe and I were in the same neighborhood babysitting co-op in San Mateo, CA, in the 1950s. She and her husband Kem had four little girls. Jim and I had four sons. Some of the children were classmates. Phoebe and I took them...one year it was eight under the age of eight...to Capitola for a week at the beach. Those weeks are among our most favorite memories.

In the 1990s, when my then husband and I could live anywhere in the world, son Matt said, "Live in Capitola, Mom. We'll bring our children to the same beach that you took us." We did and they did. For almost 20 years. Long before then Phoebe and Kem and their girls had moved to Fair Haven, NJ. Our connection was stretched taut.

As our children began to grey, Phoebe and I agreed that we needed a plan to get together. Hence, we meet each autumn on a Road Scholar trip somewhere in the United States, some place neither of us has been. This year it was St Joseph, Kansas, and Kansas City, Missouri. We learned about local art, local jazz, local bbq, and the Pony Express. As members of the group, we wore name-tags on loops around our necks. We needed to be easily identifiable. Like little refugees. Like cattle with id tags punched onto their ear flaps. Every one of the 30 of us has grey hair, some had canes, walking sticks, hiking poles. Phoebe and I, at 89, were probably the oldest, but not by much.

She and I chatted about downsizing, getting rid of our stuff. Such a popular topic in our age bracket. During my return flight, I thought about how elders puzzle over not leaving scrap books, photographs, trip journals, old tax records for our children to sort and toss. But it's hard to throw out the accumulated evidence of our lives. Our identities. Gone are the days when an adult would meet me, ask admiringly, "Aren't you Dr. Rankin's daughter?" and I'd be proud. Later, grown up, I'd hear, "Oh, it's so nice to meet Mr. Love's wife." Then, in the china department of Harrod's in London, a young woman approached and asked, "Aren't you Matt Love's mom?!"

When I was 60, I was known as a peace walker; at 80, "You're the writer, aren't you." Now? With little of my life-long context remaining, I feel as though I've lost my identity. Living in a senior community, I wonder how important our identity is. A child of God, of the Universe, of the Spirit. A grain of sand on a long, long beach.

56

TWO CHAIRS AND A TABLE

THESE CLEAR, WARM autumn days, Dottie wanders by and we sit in the sunshine, sigh as we feel our bones warming, our shoulders relaxing. We sit on the minuscule patio at my front door. Or hers. Everyone here has a place to sit outside. Our garden apartments are oriented to the outdoors. The walkways – not long hallways – connect us one to the other.

Our community is small, intimate, and unique in its architecture of single story cottages arranged along walkways that encourage a sense of neighborliness and community.

It is personal style that determines the choice of plants and arrangement of furniture on the patios. Jan has a bird-feeder attached to her front window so she can watch from inside. The shade tree in Mary's garden protects us in summer and these days drops swarms of leaves. Mary frequently calls out, "Donna! Come sit with me and tell me what you have been doing." Ruth sits quietly at a wooden table on her patio as she watches for migrating monarch butterflies.

Grandmother Sarah would have liked this place where I live. She had two chairs on her front porch where she sat rocking and calling out to passers-by, "Hello! How are you today? Come on, set a spell."

57
WANTED: A NICE CAPE

"I am fairly certain that given a cape and a nice tiara, I could save the world."

THAT'S A BRIGHT poster on 21-year-old granddaughter Katie's dresser. I am staying in her bedroom over Thanksgiving as she is in Milford Sound, New Zealand, as a crew member on the tour boat, Go Orange! A graduate in Biology and Environmental Sciences, she is prepared to share her knowledge with travelers. We here in Los Altos (south of Stanford University), spoke with Katie Thanksgiving evening. She and her new Kiwi friends had had Thanksgiving the day before in a dorm where they have private rooms, share the kitchen and the stories of their lives. "Oh, yes," she said, "outside the wind is gale force, but we're inside warm and talking up our own storm," her voice interrupted by flashes of silence. "I called to wish you happy Thanksgiving. Love you. Gotta go. Bye." Her father announced, "She's fine." Her mother smiled bravely and shrugged. Her father poured more wine. I thought of the poster on Katie's dresser.

On the other side of the world, outside Dublin, Ireland, granddaughter Indy, with a degree in Hydrology, is working with a farm family and becoming acquainted with the lifestyle there. Last summer, she started with a visit to Norway, then France, Spain, a month in Germany, and finally Ireland, and originally planned to stay abroad a year, but now with the 2016 presidential election looming in the USA, she is considering returning to help save the nation.

We elders often worry about our grandchildren's future. After the presidential election results, we were, as were millions of others, stunned into silence. Nothing much to say. Numbed as in shocked. Unable to see ahead to anything but democratic disaster, we were muted by fear.

Slowly recovering our sense of responsibility and involvement, someone asked me what I was going to do, and I said, "I have doubled my contribution to Planned Parenthood and have re-joined Sierra Club." It's not much, but every bit helps.

Also, on the Saturday after the election, I planted 21 white tulips as an act of optimism and faith.

Tomorrow, when I return to Santa Rosa, I will tell my friends of Katie's and Indy's commitments to saving the world and my faith in the younger generation.

I think I'll get myself a cape and a tiara.

58
ARE WE HAPPY YET?

WHAT DO YOU want most in life? Asked that question, many will answer, "To be happy. I want to be happy."

I've been thinking about happiness. Growing up, I was told that happiness is not a goal, it's a byproduct of living right: doing good, being kind and thoughtful. When you do those things, you'll be happy. It doesn't work if you do them in order to be happy. You are kind to be kind. You help others because you want to help others, not thinking, "If I help that person, I will get diamonds for Christmas." Only Santa Claus works that way.

In the library here last Sunday evening, I saw a 76-minute, 2011 documentary, *Happy*, directed by Academy Award nominee Roko Belic, in which people in 14 countries and various economic levels were interviewed. A rickshaw driver in India, living in what we would call poverty, is rated on the happiness scale at about the same level as the average American. All he needs is to return home at the end of the day to be greeted by the happy faces of his wife and children. Even if all they have to eat is rice , at least it's with salt.

A tour guide in Louisiana bayous spends his life in wilderness, among nature. At the end of his day, he sits in his skiff, listens to the silence and watches birds overhead. He loves where he lives and what he does. He is happy.

The United States is 23rd on the national happiness chart. Denmark is first. Some Danish happiness stems from co-op housing in which small groups share their lives. Maybe in the United States we have too much. Too much privacy, too much independence, too much loneliness. I wonder.

Since the early 1980s, the scientific measure of happiness has been recognized on a par with the psychological studies of depression. At Harvard, the class on Happiness is one of the most popular.

Michael Pritchard, a winner of San Francisco International Comedy Competition, gives students tools to make positive changes for themselves and for the school community. His goal: replace bullying with kindness.

"Our Constitution guarantees the right to pursue happiness, but you have to catch it yourself," said Benjamin Franklin. How do we do that?

In answer, I continue to source the film, *Happy*: 50% of happiness ability is based on genetic make-up, 10% is based on circumstance, i.e., job, income, social status, age, health. A whopping 40% is based on intentional behavior, actions you choose. Physical exercise is first. Being in nature "is good medicine." Add variety to life. Balance work with your personal life. Meditate. Give yourself away to a cause larger than yourself. We choose! How happy we are is, after all, our choice. It's in our attitude. In Al-Anon, twenty years ago, I first heard "Attitude of Gratitude." At first I thought it a dorky phrase, but as time went on and I became more aware of my welfare, I consciously practiced an attitude of gratitude. When I received yet another new calendar, I saved one as an extra in which I wrote what I noticed as blessings that day. Noticing has become a habit.

These days, since I moved into a senior residential facility, I am especially grateful that I can see the clouds in the sky, the moon at night. Out the back gate to a path along a creek, I watch for a pair of ducks, listen to bird-song, pick up pretty leaves. l make decisions. And that is all I ask. For enough. I tell myself I am happy.

59
LIVE AND LEARN

"AS YOU HAVE lived, so shall you age." Who said that? I've thought about it.

Have you always been a joiner? Loved board games? Lived on the edge of groups? Do you traditionally become the leader or the strong follower or someone who doesn't care to be included? Have you changed as you have aged or become even more of who you have always been?

I'm reading Anna Quindlen's memoir, *Lots of Candles, Plenty of Cake,* and on page 62, she says, "It may be that all people become more of whatever they mostly are as they grow older, the good as well as the bad, more outspoken, less inhibited, funnier, more gregarious. Sometimes it seems as though age strips away the furbelows, the accessories, and leaves just the essential person, the same way that as you get older you learn to dispense with ruffles and many buttons and just wear a black sheath dress. I had an aunt who, among other things, was known for a tongue so sharp that it sometimes qualified as a lethal weapon. As she developed dementia and her world shrank to a pinhole view, like that last frame in a Looney Tunes cartoon, she recognized no one but her husband and she lost most of her personality except for the occasional whipsaw of sharp words."

All my life I have been critical of inept authorities. As a senior in high school, I complained to the vice-principal that the English teacher couldn't even diagram sentences. By Christmas, the vice-principal herself, who had majored in English and knew grammar and how to diagram sentences, had fired the teacher and taught the class. I got an A!

When son Sam came home from 7th grade and asked what the art teacher had meant when she had said he was sexy, I was at school the next morning waiting for the principal to arrive. The art teacher was replaced.

When our eldest son Matt entered high school, I asked the principal, "Where are your bike racks?" and was told that no one rode bikes. I told him that I knew four boys who were going to be at San Mateo High School for the next nine years and they would be riding their bikes. I offered to buy a rack if he would have it installed. He declined, but the following April 22, 1970, was the first Earth Day and we got bike racks!

It should come as no surprise that I feel frustrated by some decisions made for residents here. I know nothing about managing a senior community, about budgeting, the price of operating, but nonetheless, I moan, bitch, and complain. The administration seems short-sighted and self-serving.

Now aware of the distillation, the concentration of personality and habits as we age, I'm going to pay attention during the New Year, and listen to the reasoning behind the management's edicts. This will be my 90th year. Not too late.

60
HEAR OUR VOICE

"OKAY, WHAT'LL I do with these?" A few weeks ago, I was organizing the paper pantry where I keep typing paper, colored papers, notebooks, note cards and postcards. Some are old postcards I bought when traveling in faraway places: Greece, Russia, Africa, Lake Tahoe, Cuba, Atlanta. "I'll never use these."

Or, so I thought.

Then, while some of us were playing bridge, Yvonne talked about activists who send emails to congressional representatives and sign petitions on web sites. Some telephone their representatives every day to leave messages, to say "Please..." And some send postcards.

That's it! I asked friends if they, too, had old postcards they'd probably never use. Yes, they did. Several of us collected our cards, I got three sheets of stamps, Margaret made address labels of our representatives and eight of us met for an hour or so, with tea and chocolate chip cookies, and wrote to our representatives asking them to support clean air and water, to keep fossil fuels underground, to respect women's equality and women's bodies, to protect LGBTQIA, anything that concerns us....and there is much that concerns us. We signed our names and added our zip codes so our representatives would know that we are constituents. We wrote for 90 minutes and that afternoon I dropped 60 postcards into the slot at the post office.

That was two weeks ago. Yesterday 12 of us wrote to Donald Trump. We didn't want to send hate-mail. Well, maybe we wanted to, but following Michelle Obama's insistence that "when they go low, we go high," we made constructive recommendations. Show us your tax records. Sever connections with Putin. Health-care, not wealth-care.

Pennie couldn't resist writing, "Donnie, go to your room." Then, with satisfied chuckles, some of us copied her. And helped ourselves to another Triple Ginger cookie, sipped our tea.

Dottie had bought a roll of 100 stamps and others brought what they found in their desks, and in less than two hours we were out of stamps. Over 100 postcards expressing our anxieties.

I remember Helen Caldecott, Australian pediatrician, founder of Doctors for Social Responsibility, speaking in the 1980s to a group of Stanford doctors. She said, "Your country is not a great country. It could be, but won't be until your citizens are informed and involved." Looks as though we may be getting a great country.

Yesterday morning, women in their 70s, 80s, and 90s hand-wrote postcards to the President of the United States, asking him to be a responsible leader, to be compassionate toward all. We do what we can to join the tidal wave of citizen involvement. On every card we wrote in large letters, HEAR OUR VOICE.

One evening a long time ago when I shouted to a husband, "I will be heard!" he muttered and walked away. I wonder what Trump will do. Will he hear our voice?

Does he even know that the Ides of March, March 15, when millions of postcards will arrive at his office, is the day in 44 BC that Julius Caesar received fatal knife wounds? Will he recognize this is the "Ides of Trump"?

61
HAPPY WEDNESDAY!

THIS MORNING I rolled out of bed at 6:30 so I'd have time to do the laundry. My turn in the Cluster A laundry room is seven until eleven. I opened the back door of my Rabbit Hutch, greeted a bright day, and carried the basket, glad to see purple irises blooming, the forsythia budding. We have new laundry machines, all computerized with lights and buzzers. I loaded the clothes, shut the door, poured in detergent, clicked buttons.

Nothing happened. Someone had set it for spin only and it stubbornly would do nothing but spin. Damn!

Frustrated, I gave up, returned to my bathroom, washed my hair, got dressed, made the bed, and found my glasses. Back in the laundry room, I was fumbling through the operating manual when Nancy popped in. "Ah! Nancy! Do you know how to operate this?" She did what I had done, tapped all the buttons. Finally, she pushed something that worked. Whew. Clean clothes would be ready in 55 minutes.

Back in my kitchen, I chose a bright mug, dropped a tea bag into it, and took it over to the Café for hot water. Elizabeth greeted me with, "Hey! Go get a peeled orange. Joanie is making candied orange rind for the next Bazaar and brought over a bagful of peeled oranges. They are there on the breakfast table." I took one home, broke it into sections and slurped the juiciness.

What about the eight o'clock reading group? I bet they'd like to have sections of orange.

I walked back over to the breakfast room and picked up two more oranges. Betty looked up and grinned. "Take one for each person!" I took two, broke them into a yellow bowl, and hustled over to Marie's. Contented, four of the six women stayed awake to listen to another chapter in Viking Economics.

Nice way to start the day. Lovely sense of community.

63

WATCH YOUR TONGUE

I RECENTLY HAD lunch with a friend who is searching for a compatible senior living community. She has been very diligent in checking out not only the accommodations and prices, but the continuing care options and gardening opportunities. I suggested that she check the magazines in libraries and on coffee tables to see what interests the residents. She has done that and perused libraries to note the selection of books. She has checked the activities calendars. How about yoga and pilates and exercises?

She has asked about the political preferences of the voters in residence. Are there any activists? Do they participate in local demonstrations or send postcards to their representatives? She has asked about vegetarian, vegan, dairy-free and gluten-free meals. She wants to know about housekeeping and linen services.

Is there a chapel on the premises?

Is a doctor available? What happens when a person falls? How many assisted living apartments? Who maintains the gardens at the front doors of cottages? What if I want to paint a wall a color other than Navajo White?

What is the turnover of the staff members? I never thought to ask this, but see the wisdom of it. If employees are happy with their work conditions, they stay, and they are happy with the residents, and that raises the morale of everyone. It creates a sense of security and continuity. I was beginning to realize that a sense of security and continuity was important to me. Administration needs to be steady, smart, sophisticated, and sincere.

My friend shared with me that she considered a particular senior community until someone told her that the residents are prone to gossip and to being catty. I realized then that here gossip does not exist. We might talk about someone, but only with concern. "I think Patty is depressed since her cat died. What can we do for her?" or "Did you hear that Paul is in hospice now?"

However, we are not perfect. I heard one woman say, "She wears me out with her self-importance!" I watched to see reactions until someone said gently, "Oh, let her live her life – and you live yours." And we moved on to other subjects. I find this compassion, patience, and acceptance touching and reassuring. It speaks of the quality of the population here.

I think that song "People" says it well. "People who love people are the luckiest people in the world."

Remember Thumper's mother told him, "If you can't say anything nice, don't say anything at all." With the variety of cottages and apartments, services and meals, directors and staff, as I've said repeatedly, I think that the most important facet of living in a senior community is the quality of the residents. Ones who share their hearts and watch their tongues.

64

TWO WOMEN FARMERS

ISAK DINESEN, ALSO known as Karen Blixen, was a fine storyteller and an example of a woman who followed her convictions. I was thirteen years old when my father gave me a copy of her book, *Out of Africa*. Since reading that book, I have held her in high esteem. When she lived in Kenya in the early 20th century, she became, in addition to an author, a coffee grower. The opening sentence in her book is, "I have a farm in Africa at the foot of the Ngong Hills."

In the 1990s I had a farm in Oregon, near Elkton in the Coastal Range. And like Isak/Karen, I was married to a charming man. I loved the rural life and built a small cabin above the Umpqua River where I wrote little stories. I think she and I each asked too much of our marriages. Neither lasted.

I clung to the similarities between my life and that of Isak Dinesen's.

Then I left the farm and moved to the beach in Santa Cruz County and didn't think about her very much and the years passed. Now, in a senior community in Santa Rosa, I will be 90 in September and think about being old. What does that mean? Will I be a burden to my family? Will my life begin to revolve around doctor appointments? Will I become creaky? disillusioned? grouchy and picky? Will my life narrow and my perspective diminish? These are what elders often dwell upon.

Then, suddenly, when I was least expecting it, I ran across this quote from Isak Dinesen! She said, "Women, when they are old enough to have done with the business of being women, and can let loose their strength, must be the most powerful creatures in the world."

Just in the nick of time!

I'm determined to make the next ten to fourteen years the best they can be. Like Isak, when confronted by a massive lion in the bush, when I face depressing thoughts, I will wave my hands and say, "Shoo. Shoo."

65

GARDENS

THE GARDENS I see this year are better than I've ever seen them. The rewards of copious amounts of rain? Yes, I think so, but we also are fortunate to have a new gardening crew. Gardeners who know how to prune and trim and allow bushes to look like bushes instead of tortured constricted balls. Antonio spends entire days selectively weeding, and other days spreading mulch and tidying up the edges of flower beds. We residents reap the benefits of his expertise and gentle approach to the plants living here with us.

Secondly, resident Ginny's son Eric has helped improve our landscape. Last year for Clare, he designed and planted a new garden that included a bird feeder and plants to attract butterflies. He planted a low-maintenance garden for his mom; then designed for others, and then for me. He pulled and chopped and pick-axed at the little space out my back door, leaned on his shovel, and asked, "What do you envision here?"

I told him white, yellow, peachy colors. No blue or pink. "Lavender is okay. I'd like the garden to be loose, and blowzy. A cottage garden that will be drought-tolerant just in case the weather turns dry again." He planted Queen Anne's Lace, Mrs. Geum, feverfew, salvia, several lavenders, a couple of day lilies, and a show-stopper red dahlia. I added Shasta daisies, a small rose, sweet peas, and 21 white tulips.

The tulips shoved up and burst forth just as the Queen Anne's lace nodded and bloomed and the feverfew began. A lovely moon white garden. When the white garden faded, we saw a controlled chaos of color. Sweet peas, the color of watermelon, 10 feet tall. Yellows and oranges everywhere. Big red poppies, a struggling little apricot rose. The dahlia had died in the winter frost.

My garden reflects my passion for color and surprise and freedom. Other gardens reflect their owners. Lynn's is as meditative as she is; Charlotte's displays her talent at arranging. Maureen's shows her sense of energy and myriad enthusiasms. Lynn has a garden that mirrors her sense of organization and tidiness.

Some gardens are sloppy, but so are their owners. I find them, both the gardens and their people, painful and pathetic. Some gardens have little tiny plants arranged precisely by their daintily precise creators. Some gardens, those belonging to people who would prefer to sit inside and read, are minimalist, getting along as best they can with occasional watering and rare weeding.

I've thought about gardens and their philosophical significance and could devote my entire life to that study. It seems to me that gardens inform human thinking about mortality, order, and power. Also, I think, gardens refer to eternity, the cycle of life and death and the beauty of each phase. The delicate Queen Ann Lace blossoms faded into dry frilly seed heads, wonderful in dried flower arrangements.

Gardens seem to be a metaphor for the human condition. Can it be true that as we tend our gardens, so do we tend our lives?

66

MOVING ON

I ANSWERED THE door to find a woman with a clipboard and a big smile. "Hi," she said, "I'm here to talk about your move. We will be moving you July 13," and she handed me her card.

"Oh, yes. Come in," I said and stepped aside to let her pass. As she sat down on the sofa, she looked around, nodded, and said, "Two rooms and a bath. Should take three of us the day, July 12, to get everything packed up and ready to go. Mind if I open your cupboards?" I thought she just wanted to see what was inside, but she took pictures with her phone and told me, "When we get to your new place, we'll unbox your things and put them away as close as we can to your design here." She added, "The truck and truckers will be here Thursday morning. When you get up, take the covers off the bed so they can put it on the truck."

My new place? Yes, I'm moving. To Spring Lake Village, another senior living community about four miles from here. They arranged for the packers and movers. This is the first time I've had professional movers. Piece o' cake!

I like much about the place where I've been living: love the residents, admire the ethics and generosity and intellectual prowess of those who are my neighbors. I appreciate the gardens and the greens and the trees. The architecture is inspired with recessed front doors, little front patios where I sit to read or eat breakfast or pet one of the cats who live here or just to soak up the sunshine and talk with friends who pause as they pass by. I will miss all this.

But I need to know services will be available for any contingency. I abhor the idea of someone else deciding if and when I need to be moved. I'll decide for myself. I may never need memory care, but I want to know it is available just in case. I need stability and reassurance. In the three years I've been here, we have had four executive directors. Each with ideas that seem to agitate the residents. I want the next 10 or so years to be secure and fun with as few worries and concerns as possible.

I think I will feel cared for at Spring Lake Village. The other day the phone rang and a woman I didn't know said, "This is Randi from linens. What size bed do you have?" I thought she was a linen-store salesperson. But, no, she continued with, "On Thursday, July 13, we will bring sheets and make your bed. I want to know the size we should bring." I was pleased. She wasn't through. "We'll bring your towels, too. They are a nice cream color. You'll like them." She explained that each week the cleaning lady would change the bed and hang fresh towels. I'm liking this kind of service!

Bea has been in marketing at Spring Lake Village for 23 years. Dennis in maintenance, has been here a dozen or so years. With infinite patience and thoroughness, they each have answered my questions, and my son Sam's questions. Patrice, who guides new residents through initial steps of acclimation, read out loud to me, as I read in my copy, the entire contract and along the way, paused to ask if I had a question. She read to me for 45 minutes.

When I first moved to the first senior residence over three years ago, I was excited about the new adventure. But I had moved with not enough caution. I should have asked more questions. I needed more transparency and consistency. Now I know that confidence comes with experience. This time I have no downsizing, I am taking everything. I am sure Spring Lake Village is a better choice for me. I'm moving on.

67

STORAGE

Mary Oliver

When I moved from one house to another
there were many things I had no room
for. What does one do? I rented a storage
space. And filled it. Years passed.
Occasionally I went there and looked in,
but nothing happened, not a single
twinge of the heart.

As I grew older the things I cared
about grew fewer, but were more
important. So one day I undid the lock
and called the trash man. He took
everything.

I felt like the little donkey when
his burden is finally lifted. Things!
Burn them burn them! Make a beautiful
fire! More room in your heart for love,
for the trees! For the birds who own
nothing – the reason they can fly.

68

I DON'T NEED MUCH

YEARS AGO, ONCE Upon a Time….., a visiting friend turned to me and inquired, "Are we going to have lunch?"

"Oh," I jumped up. "Of course!" and flung myself into the kitchen.

He called after me, "I don't need much, but I want it to be very good."

I thought of that recently when I met and talked with some Spring Lake Village guests who were here to attend a promotional event. Several of us residents stood to speak about various reasons we enjoy SLV. I spoke about first impressions, including my delight with Betsy-the-Move-In woman and her crew. I've mentioned before that a month or so before my moving date, Betsy appeared at my front door, clipboard and pen in hand. She breezed in, sat down, looked around, and asked if she could take pictures. Yes, of course. I thought she was photographing how much stuff I had. She opened the cupboards and closets to take pictures.

On moving day, the crew appeared, boxed and trucked everything over to SLV. They placed the furniture according to my directions, unloaded the boxes into cupboards and closets, took the boxes away, and wished me a happy future.

That evening, four members of my family came to have a glass of wine before walking to the dining room. I was in. A good first impression. One worth sharing. But now I think I might have talked about the fact that, like my friend at lunch, I don't need much, but I want it to be very good.

I don't need much square footage in my cottage; 700 is fine. I do appreciate the quality of the cupboards, the heft of the handles, that the cupboard doors hang plum. I like the crown molding, the careful mitering of the corners. In the bedroom, the sliding closet doors glide smoothly and the mirrors are beveled. The installation of the tiles in the bathroom is meticulous. The subway tiles of the back-splash in the kitchen are good as are the appliances, including the heart-winning 18" dishwasher.

I admire the paneled front door and the rhododendrons and azaleas near the walk.

I don't need an acre of garden such as I had on the farm in Oregon. Here the back 40 – that's 40 feet – is plenty for a rose bush, some grasses and daisies and the yellow bench.

On the tiny patio, I can sit in the patch of sunshine, gaze at a glimpse of the sky, and be grateful for underground telephone and electric wires. If I need a broader view, I walk along the roadways around the campus.

In the central dining room the portions served are smaller than in restaurants and are presented with a sprig of parsley, a sprinkling of chopped nuts, or a shaving of Parmesan. As granddaughter Jenny followed me into the dining room her first noontime here, she asked, "Gran, is the food at Spring Lake Village good?" I took her hand and asked, "How many times did I ask you to lunch in the other senior center where I lived?" She chuckled. As we sat down and looked at the menu, I reminded her that if she wanted to order double, just do it. I have a friend here who always orders double steamed spinach.

I've told Jenny the story that I've just told you about my friend who wanted not much, but he wanted it to be very good.

69
OUTTA HERE!

IS THIS WHAT it feels like to be a refugee, homeless, without some basic
necessities? In fact, I am an evacuee from Santa Rosa.

October 9, 2017, Monday pre-dawn, I wakened to the sound of gongs. A
deep authoritative voice (the voice of God?) intoned, "This is not a drill.
Repeat. This is not a drill." I sat up. "This is an emergency evacuation. Meet at
your Emergency Bench." I rushed to push my feet into Birkenstocks, grabbed
a sweatshirt and flashlight, and, still in my pajamas, started out the door.
Stop! Catching myself in this panicked motion, I retreated into the house and
shut the door. Not everyone is going to react so quickly. I needn't hurry.

Back into the bedroom, I sat on the side of the bed, then put on
yesterday's pair of pants, put on a t shirt and sweatshirt, didn't care if my
socks were color-coordinated, and tied the laces on walking shoes. Grabbed a
nice shopping bag from behind the door and headed for the bathroom.
Brushed my teeth. Dropped the toothbrush into the bag. Washed and dried
my face and dropped the towel into the bag. Remembered to include
toothpaste. Brushed my hair, added the hair brush. Moved to the kitchen and
opened the refrigerator door, and took out what was in front: half a loaf of
cinnamon bread, a block of cheese, an apple, two small containers of orange
juice, and my water bottle. Added a sharp knife and the iPhone. Picked up the

flashlight and bag, turned out the lights, considered watering the house plants, and walked out the door over to the Emergency Bench.

Others were gathering. Some with pets, a gentleman in his plaid bathrobe, several with walkers. We studied the pre-dawn sky: to the East, a dark gray and to the north a pulsing pink. "Something's wrong," said the man in the plaid bathrobe. Our volunteer resident warden checked our names, some offered to drive to the Sonoma County Fairgrounds, our evacuee shelter, a few miles away. I chose to be among Jack's passengers, because Jack looked big and healthy and capable and maybe in his mid-70s. Jack's mother and my neighbor Dorothy came, too.

Once in the vast parking lot, we spilled out of cars, milled around with others we recognized, checked the sky. Same ominous gray and pink. Someone said, "We are surrounded by forest fires. Those 50-mile-an-hour winds last night whipped flames from one ridge to the next."

At the entry to the main building, we signed in, sat at long tables, sipped water or coffee, ate small oranges and large Costco muffins, chatted, reassured each other. At the end of one table, four people played bridge. I was impressed with the general demeanor of the SLV residents: calm, cooperative, helpful, mildly cheerful, appreciative.

One worried woman leaned toward me and said, "I am not comfortable here. I hope we don't have to stay long." I, ever the cheerleader, reminded her that we were safe and dry. We had warm water, clean bathrooms, outlets to charge our iPhones, food, medications, and people to care for us. And we had each other. She looked resigned and said, "Well, as long as we don't have to sleep here." I didn't point out to her that at the other end of huge space, cots were arriving.

My son Sam and his wife Sandra, in northeast Santa Rosa, had mandatory evacuation around two o'clock Monday morning. They ran to their horses and loaded them into the trailer. Sandra drove the truck/trailer, Sam drove the family car with Bubba the dog, and Sandra's mother Betty drove her car to the parking lot at the fairgrounds. They took very little from their house. Not even Sam's beautiful new guitar.

At the fairgrounds, they found me among the SLV residents! A miracle! Sandra said, "Look at that sky. Darker and darker. I want outta here. We're going to a friend's ranch near Sebastopol. Want to come with us?" I was tempted, just to be together, but by then, I was expecting son John and Holly who were driving up from Los Altos (SF peninsula) to rescue me from the dust- and ash-laden air.

When John and Holly arrived, I signed out and we drove back to Spring Lake Village where John collected the computer, address books, and calendar from the desk. Holly closed the windows, collected food from the refrigerator, reminded me to take the vitamins and hearing aids (which I, in my pre-dawn haste, had forgotten), and I jammed some clothes and necessities into a bag.

John drove my car and I climbed in with Holly, counted my blessings, and we were outta there.

The first step in a long process. Now what'll we do?

70
WHAT A WEEK!

"WHAT A WEEK!" my Santa Rosa son Sam said.

In the dark about 2 a.m. on Monday, October 9, he and his wife Sandra were wakened by shouting, "Evacuate now!" They grabbed their passports, other documents, loaded the two horses in to the trailer and fled to the huge open parking lot of the Sonoma County Fairgrounds.

About nine o'clock that morning, in the main exhibition hall, they found me among evacuees from Spring Lake Village. I count that as the miracle of the day. Not that they found me, but that we were all at the fairgrounds. Later, after a pasta and salad lunch, brought by Community Services, I looked up to see Sam's brother John and his wife Holly striding toward me. We drove carefully back to SLV to retrieve my car and some possessions and headed to their home in Los Altos, two hours south of Santa Rosa.

Sam and Sandra had taken the horses and Bubba the dog out to friends who board horses on their ranch near Sebastopol and slept three nights there.

More than 1,700 homes are lost and 17,000 acres are scorched. It is a tragedy beyond comprehension.

During the week of October 9 to 16, Sharon York, Executive Director of Spring Lake Village, delivered daily updates at two o'clock on Facebook. I clung to the human interest stories. One was of the 11 cats still wandering around SLV. They were being fed, watered, and petted. Dennis, head of the maintenance department, had taken a pet bird, Felix, in his cage, with his cover, home with him.

In the early part of the week, I noticed I couldn't get warm. My hands, feet, and ears were cold even though I had plenty of clothing during the days and warm blankets at night. Older people are often cold and keep their homes overly warm. I wondered if that was happening to me. Then, later in the week, I realized the weather had not changed. But I was warm again. "Must be that you were in some shock, Donna," a friend surmised. Maybe so.

I was sleepy every afternoon and hardly awake enough in the evening to put on my pajamas. But in bed, I was restless, unable to sleep well. By Saturday, I was back to alert days and drowsing nights. What was that all about?

A smart friend asked me for details of the fire. I talked and talked and talked and finally apologized for rattling on so long. She shook her finger at me, "You must talk about this. This is a trauma that must heal and talking about it is an important way to do that." I asked if that could explain the veterans of WWII having always to talk about The War. "Absolutely!" she said. So whenever anyone has asked, I have talked about the fire, the smoke, the uprooting of 450 elderly residents of Spring Lake Village, some in their bathrobes.

I notice, too, that I repeat myself in writing about those first days of the evacuation.

After a few days in Los Altos, I drove over the hill to Aptos in Santa Cruz County, to visit son Matt, his wife Joan, and their James. Each morning, I assessed the clarity of the sky and found that the color blue had never been more lovely. No wonder the Virgin Mary wears a blue gown. The air quality in Sonoma County is being compared to that of Beijing, the worst in the world.

My friend Joanie, who lives in the Santa Rosa senior community named Friends House, was staying with one of her children in Woodside, on the SF Peninsula. We met at noon one day midway between us, in Pescadero to have lunch and to talk about how the Santa Rosa fires have affected us. She and I have traveled to Cuba and Iceland together. We are dependable friends. When I saw her crossing the street to meet me, my heart swelled. My 92-year-old friend with her handsome cane and brightly flowered vest saw me and smiled her wide smile and we talked for three hours! Mostly we appreciated our good fortune in the midst of devastation: our residences are still standing and we have loving supportive families. We compared our evacuation experiences, recent sleep patterns, tensions, blood pressures, and emotional states. We both admitted feeling guilty, but decided "we can't help anyone right now but we will when we return." I came away from that conversation feeling much more grounded.

Yesterday Sam called. When he asked what I was doing, I told him I was sitting in my car in the parking lot next to Tonic Salon in downtown Santa Cruz and, "I just got my hair cut."

"Me, too," he chuckled. "I guess things are getting back to normal."

71
UP FROM THE ASHES

THE FIRST TIME I heard that phrase "up from the ashes," I was nine years old. In 1936, the town of Bandon, 18 miles down river from our Coquille, in southwestern Oregon, burned. The Irish Furze (Gorse) was pitchy and brittle and the winds high. My parents' friends came to our house with what they could retrieve from their homes, and stayed for a while. After the fire, I heard them talking about rebuilding up from the ashes.

Now, after the fires that ripped through neighborhoods of Santa Rosa, I hear that phrase again. It will take years to recover. The immediate need is to find housing for thousands of homeless people. People who have lost everything!

We 450 residents of Spring Lake Village who were evacuated within one and a half hours on the morning of Monday, October 9, are back. Everything here looks just as nice, just as orderly and cheerful as it did a month ago, before the fires. The emphasis is on the well-being of those of us who live here. Yesterday in the monthly Transitions meeting, we told our stories. What happened, what we did, what we thought and felt.

What we are feeling now? What was difficult for us and what would we have done if SLV had burned? The minute that question was asked, one woman teared up. She told us she had moved here in September, only a few weeks before the fire. She found a nice boarding stable for her horse, and was adjusting well to her new life. She had not yet heard of the emergency drills, the to-go bag. She had noticed the benches designated as gathering places in case of emergency. The evacuation and her concern for her horse were traumatic and she hadn't once thought of what would happen if she lost everything.

One man said that if SLV had burned, he would consider moving to Bali, or better yet, to Thailand. He and his wife like the weather there. He said the food is good and they have friends in Thailand. I was cheered by his remarks; I had thought if I had to, I'd go to Alamos, Sonora, Mexico, at least until I had things figured out.

Which of my lost belongings would I mourn? Actually, sentimental as I am over my family treasures, I probably would be fine without them. I might collect the insurance and just live on cruise ships for the next 10 to 14 years. Come back whenever a new great-grandchild was born. And for Christmas. One Christmas I tried being away and spent more than an hour sitting in the tropical sun on a friend's patio steps, talking on the phone to family.

What was hard during this time of recovery from the evacuation? Sleepless nights, bad dreams, weepiness, lack of ability to focus, increased appetite for ice cream.

I had asked a friend what was difficult for her. She had sighed and told me, "The other day, I had a hard time maneuvering the (golf) cart. There were so many downed leaves and little branches left from the winds that scattered the fires, I could barely go." She leaned toward me, put her hand on my arm for emphasis, and scowled. "I almost couldn't get to the thirteenth tee." I had thought of the enormous losses suffered by so many and could only look at her without comment.

What changes have we noticed in ourselves? Many spoke of their increased awareness and gratitude for safe family and friends. One noticed how much brighter and lovelier the autumn leaves seem this year. Some feel guilty for their good fortune and have become compulsively involved in helping others. One cheerful woman told of agencies warehousing and distributing clothing and household supplies that have flooded in from local residents and merchants.

Toward the end of our Transitions meeting, one resident offered, "There are changes and there are transitions. When we allow the changes to change us, we are transitioned. I think that is what has happened with us."

Someone else offered, "Remember when our three-year-old children would lean into our leg and grab hold? They did that when they were confused or hurt or in some way needed our strength. I think that we have leaned closer to God."

72

YOU HAVE CHOICES

"FOLLOW YOUR BLISS. Doors will open and guides will appear."
Remember Joseph Campbell saying that? Everyone I knew was much younger
then and many applied it to choosing careers or life partners or identifying
their passions.

Recently a 20-something granddaughter and I had a long conversation
about the choices she has and how she will make them. She spoke of her job
that she loves, the co-workers who have become real friends, her pride in the
quality of the product. It provides well for her. Seemingly perfect, except she
knows the job now and the challenge is no longer there. Should she try
something else?

I thought of my father's answer when I asked him what he thought I
should major in. First he said, "Take pre-med. Can't hurt. Might help." The
following year, when I got a D in a five-hour chemistry class, he said, "Do
what you love. The money will follow." I majored in psychology and have
been glad ever since. Worked in the psych department at University of
Oregon, taught at Sarah Dix Hamlin School in San Francisco, loved bringing
up four sons while I held a copy of Gesell and Ilg (a child development
resource) in the other hand, led troubled tutorial students to success, wrote
some books, and in Saturday workshops, shared my enthusiasm for writing.
Psych helped.

Here at Spring Lake Village, I had lunch last week with a new friend and we told bits of our life stories. She explained that yes, she, too, had taught school, but became tired of controlling restless adolescents. Quilting calmed and refreshed her. Loving to quilt, she shared her passion in Adult Education classes. So rewarding to be teaching students who wanted to learn! But frequently she found she needed something that she'd left at home. And her students had the same frustrating experience. So she found a storefront, opened a quilting store, taught classes there and whenever she or a student needed something, they could find it on the store shelves. She loved her quilting career.

She no longer has the store, but continues to exhibit her quilts in art shows. I asked her if she had made any money when she had owned the store and taught. She shrugged a little and smiled, "Not a lot, but enough."

That's it! Enough! She had followed her bliss and look what happened.

Saturday afternoon three of us senior residents drove over to see a model train set up in a house. The "engineer" has a complex arrangement in the garage. Historically correct mines and warehouses, a church, a hardware store, an Out West neighborhood. Not only in the garage, but in the dining room as well. In the kitchen, looking for a water glass, I opened a cupboard and found it full of small buildings not quite ready to be set out along the tracks. I asked the engineer's wife, "You two live at Spring Lake Village, don't you? Who lives here?"

She explained that no one lives there. Sometimes family members come stay over, but the house is for the trains. "My husband used the second bedroom at Spring Lake Village to set up this section," indicating a 12-foot long, waist-high display of buildings, mountains and tracks, "but then ran out of space." She went on, "This is our solution. Real estate is not a bad investment and trains are Bill's passion. This gets him up in the mornings. He's 91 now and still has a boy's love for toy trains."

I like these reminders that we almost always have choices. At any time during our lives, some way, somehow, we can follow our bliss.

73

IT'S A SURPRISE A MINUTE

I HAD NOTICED Bev in exercise class. She is trim and tidy in her jeans and cashmere sweaters, her face carefully tended, and her posture erect. One day we introduced ourselves and asked the usual questions. "Where have you lived the major part of your life?" she asked.

"San Mateo. I lived in San Mateo area for about 40 years. I last lived in San Mateo Park."

"Oh," she said, "I lived in San Mateo Park. Where did you live?"

"Occidental Avenue. I have forgotten the house number. What about you?"

She squinted into the past and answered, "I can't remember. Oh, well."

The class started. We didn't talk about our other lives any more.

Until last week. Bev and her husband sat behind me at the Wednesday evening concert and she tapped me on the shoulder. I turned around and she said, "526 Occidental Avenue."

Surprised, I said, "That's right! How did you know my address?"

"No," she smiled. "That was my address."

I chuckled through the entire concert. At its conclusion, Bev and I compared notes. The dog run along the side of the house, the pool in the backyard, the bonus room downstairs. She said, "I had barely put the house on the market and some woman came by, walked around, and said she would buy it."

I nodded. She said, "You got a very good deal."

Those who know me, know I love Small World Stories. I think I've already written that up until last week, my favorite one was about the time I was standing a long time in the china department of Harrods in London. I was waiting to be helped so when a pleasant looking young woman approached me, I said, "I'm glad to see you. I'd like to buy Peter Rabbit mugs" and hadn't finish my sentence before she said, "I don't work here. Aren't you Matt Love's mom! We were in San Mateo High together."

I think we all have these stories. They seem especially prevalent here in Spring Lake Village. I was telling about Bev's and my having lived in the same house on Occidental, and my walking buddy stopped and said, "My grandmother lived in the 600 block of Occidental Avenue in San Mateo Park."

74

SERVICE WITH SMILES

PEOPLE ASK ME why I like Spring Lake Village, the senior community where I've lived for six months now. I have several answers. I like the stability of the administration. I am grateful for the extensive medical services available. I like the food and I am tickled by the consideration and respect that members of the staff exhibit. For the 400 or so of us residents there are 275 employees and all seem dedicated to giving good service.

I'll give you an example. It happened today at lunch time. Six of us women were seated at a round table in the Bistro. Our waitress took our orders. I asked for a bowl of fresh fruit and a 10-inch Margherita pizza.

Nina's veggie-burger arrived. Joyce's soup came. Bev's huge chicken sandwich looked daunting. Selma's Caesar Salad had whole anchovies! My strawberries, cantaloupe, and melon appeared. No pizza.

After a while, I asked the waitress, "Should I expect the pizza soon?" She disappeared, and returned to apologize for the delay, explained that the first pizza had been burned and a second one was being prepared. She smiled and vanished. The chef came to our table and explained that the fire "got pretty hot," apologized and with the bright smile of a good idea, he asked, "Would you like some french fries or Bistro Chips?" I love the chips so accepted. They came, warm, fragrant, spicy and we all enjoyed them.

Then the waitress re-appeared and placed a slice of cheese cake in front of me. "Here, This is for you. I am so sorry that you are having to wait." She cleared away some of the others' dishes.

Finally the pizza came. Fresh and tempting. I ate one piece, asked for a box, "and a box for the cheese cake, too, please." Bev said, "Here, Donna, take home the rest of these chips. I know what you'll be having for dinner tonight."

We stood up to leave. The chef waived, smiled and nodded. The waitress stepped back out of our way and said, "Good bye, Ms. Love. Thank you."

I almost hugged her. "Thank you. See you tomorrow."

75

IF NOT NOW, WHEN?

LAST MONTH, THE leader of the Spring Lake Village Drumming Circle mentioned that she is taking a group of nine women to Costa Rica to drum in the Living Forest, a retreat center near Lake Arenal, within sight of Arenal Volcano. She spoke of drumming with monkeys, butterflies, and grade-school children. A float trip on the Tenario River for bird-watching, bathing in Llanos Cortes waterfalls, and walks in the jungle were too tempting. Could I resist?

I've wanted for 30 years to go to Costa Rica. I've wanted to see how not having a standing army affects the quality of life. What happens when monies can be diverted to schools, hospitals, and social services? How do people feel when the word "guns" is not part of daily conversation? I wanted to see why Costa Rica is among the three top places in the world rated as the happiest. So I signed up.

Cautious friends have warned me that it's tropical, only ten degrees north of the equator, which means high temperatures (80's and 90's), high humidity (60%), and maybe bugs. I melt into a puddle in hot sticky weather and studiously avoid mosquitoes that leave me with welts the size of the bowls of cream soup spoons and long, itchy, sleepless nights. But I'm going!

Granddaughter Katie who spends as much time outdoors as she can, said, "Gran, go to REI and get their best mosquito repellent." I did and asked the clerk why he recommended a particular tube. He said, "My wife gets big welts from bug bites and she uses this. It works." I bought it. Then he handed me another tube of ointment for itchy bites. "Just in case," he said. I'm set.

A cardiologist suggested I postpone this trip, or not go at all. She pointed out that I am 90 now and she is worried about an irregular heartbeat, but a couple of years ago another cardiologist emphasized, "You have a regular irregular heartbeat. Don't worry about it." I'm not.

Sunday, March 11, about three o'clock in the morning, after we have set our clocks an hour ahead, I will be picked up here at Spring Lake Village on the front curb and several of us will drive out to the Santa Rosa airport and fly to Los Angeles en route to Liberia, Costa Rica.

Imagine me! The girl who wanted to play timpani drums in the high school orchestra and never did, finally going to play West African drums in the jungle of Costa Rica!

If not now, when?

76

HABIT OF LIVING

"THE LONG HABIT of living indisposeth us for dying." Sir Thomas Browne (1605-1682) said that.

I like it.

Life in a senior community includes daily allusions to death. One friend worries about Spring Lake Village expansion and another says, "I don't care. By the time they add more units, I won't be here. They can have my apartment. I'll be dead."

I had tiles added to my patio floor. "How long will they last?" The contractor replied, "At least 10 years." Fine, that's long enough for me.

A friend tells me, "I just got my driver's license renewed. Good for five years. It'll still be good after I'm gone. Hope the car lasts as long as I do."

These comments are said not with morbidity or resignation, but with acceptance. Little asides spoken between ordering from the menu and the arrival of iced tea.

These days I devote more time to taking care of my body than I did 50 years ago. In those days, I had a yearly check-up with the doctor – THE doctor – and with the dentist. Now I have the primary doctor and all the specialists. A healthy 90-year-old and in my card file I have one for the SLV primary care doctor; two cardiologists, one more specialized than the other; an acupuncturist, a vitreoretinal consultant, an optometrist, a pediatric orthopedist, a dermatologist, dentist (DDS, MS, RN), an oral surgeon, urologist, and a head & neck specialist.

Last week as I drove home from an appointment with a new doctor, I felt really happy that I'd found one I like and who took time to listen to concerns and answer questions. Buoyant, I laughed at myself that this is what was making me happy: finding a doctor I liked! How different from the 20-year-old me finding a new boyfriend or a new salmon-colored cardigan sweater. Very different from the pleasure of making a birthday cake from scratch that turned out rich and pretty. When we must devote more time to caring for our aging bodies, finding a compassionate doctor gives great pleasure.

What else in this life brings me joy? The garden. The small cottage garden I've created with a yellow bench, a yellow rose, lavenders, and seven yellow yarrow plants scattered among the bushes that were here when I moved in. Early in the morning, still in pajamas, I go out into the garden to deadhead spent blossoms, to clip, nip, admire, and encourage.

At the front door, I found a bag of small canning jars left for me by a neighbor who knows I still like making berry jam and applesauce.

I admired son Sam as he returned the folded chairs to their storage niche after five of us had sat together on the patio.

I introduced a friend and a granddaughter and watched her young graciousness and poise.

I like the bright smiles and firm, confident hand-shakes that the doctors offer.

Little things. Things that the long habit of living allows me to notice and savor.

77

HARVEST TIME

HENRY WADSWORTH LONGFELLOW observed,

> For age is opportunity no less
> Than youth itself, though in another dress.
> And as the evening twilight fades away
> The sky is filled with stars, invisible by day.

I read that in Joan Chittister's *The Gift of Years*, subtitled. "Growing Older Gracefully." It is a treasure of a book, given to me last year for my 90th birthday by a friend I've known since she was a college girl and I was a busy mother of four young boys. I am constantly surprised that she is in her 70s now and considering moving into a senior community. I can't be too surprised, though, since those young boys are now in their early 60s.

Longfellow continues speaking of the mystery of the later years of life, the satisfaction of it all. "And yet one of the obstacles to living an exciting life in our later years is that we become so sure we're losing something and so unaware of what we're gaining."

He says, "the later years of life are given to us to bring in the harvest of all that effort" that we spent during young and middle years. I recently visited a friend who bought a house on the shore of Indian Lake in Michigan to spend summers near her grandchildren. As a parent, Louise devoted her life to her children and is being rewarded by adoring grandchildren. An important part of her harvest.

My own grandchildren are adults now, some having babies of their own. And I reap the benefits of dedicated motherhood. Bringing in the harvest. When we think of harvest, we think of corn, of garden produce. Louise and I drove to Mr. Sprague's farm stand to gather peaches, tomatoes, a white aubergine, apples, corn, and small red potatoes. Three generations of the Sprague family worked the busy money box. Reaped the benefits of hard work, their harvest.

No wonder autumn is my favorite season. No wonder that as I age, I feel more and more comfortable with the soft days of contemplation. I frequently sit in the sun on the yellow garden bench and just listen to the hum of silence. Yesterday I sat very still to watch a neighborhood cat stand on her hind legs to drink from the bird bath. A crow teetered on the bird feeder, made it swing until most of the seeds had fallen to the ground, and then flapped down to the path to snap up lunch. The cat ran away. A monarch butterfly almost landed on my hand, but decided to choose the buddleia bush. Bees hovered over the lavender, and a hummingbird liked the agapanthus. I felt almost as though I were in Eden. Nothing else demanded attention. I was present. In the garden.

Since being in Michigan for two weeks, in airports and train stations, in traffic, in the mainstream, I have felt that life at Spring Lake Village is not a real life. It feels like Shangri La or Never-Never land.

But that is not so. This is my real life. This cocoon, this padded, quiet, safe and sanitary life is the real life of the seniors who live here. I understand now that there are parallel lives. This is one of them. And it's autumn. Time to harvest.

78
THIS IS NOT THE END

REMEMBER THOSE OLD knock-knock jokes? Knock knock. Who's there? Dishes. Dishes who? Dishes de end.

Wrong. This is not the end. I plan to continue to write blogs about living well and aging well in a community we call home. You can find the blogs at donnarankinlove.wordpress.com.

ACKNOWLEDGEMENTS

One evening in early 2018, I mentioned that several people had suggested that the blogs I'd been writing for a few years be made into a book. "It would be a guide for elders and their families when they are looking for a senior living community."

I was pleased with the idea, but thought it'd be too much work. Granddaughter Jenny Love, a professional photographer in her late twenties, offered, "I could make the blogs into a book. Gran, you send me the words as you'd like them to be in a book, and I'll do the rest."

I thank Phyllis Gallaway and John Love for expert editing. Director of Marketing at Spring Lake Village, Judy Haley, gave encouragement at exactly the right time. Hugs to graphic designer and grandson, Derek Love, for his consult on the cover design. And to granddaughter Jenny Love goes my eternal gratitude and admiration for taking on this project, for the cover design, for her patience and perseverance. I wrote the blogs. She birthed the book.

From blogs to book, but only with help and enthusiasm from my friends and family.

It's been fun, Jenny,

Donna Rankin Love
March 16, 2019

ABOUT THE AUTHOR

Since turning 80, Donna Rankin Love has written and previously published three books of stories based on her rich and varied life. Raising four sons. Remodeling houses in Mexico. Running a tutoring center for dyslexic students. Walking across America in the Great Peace March for Nuclear Disarmament.

She continues to write blogs. To people who are intimidated by writing their lives, she says, "Write your lives one tale at a time. Remember, you don't have to start at the beginning!"

Made in the USA
Columbia, SC
31 July 2019